The
Advertising Research Handbook

The
Advertising
Research Handbook

by
Charles E. Young

FIRST EDITION
Ideas in Flight
Seattle, Washington
a division of Ad Essentials, LLC.

First Edition April, 2005

ISBN 0-9765574-0-1

The author is grateful for permission to use exhibit material from Unilever, Sara Lee, and Hello Hello, Inc.

Front Page Cover Photo
Physicist Harold Edgerton used stop-action photography to freeze time and make the invisible visible. © Harold & Esther Edgerton Foundation, 2005, courtesy of Palm Press, Inc.

Back Page Cover Art
The Ameritest Flow of Attention graph freezes time to study how audience attention flows through the moving pictures of film.

Illustrations, cover and book layout and design by Patricia D. Deering.

Printed in the United States of America.

Contents

FOREWORD IX

INTRODUCTION XI

I. A Short History of TV Copytesting 1
The Report Card Measures: Filtering the
   Creative
The Role of Diagnostics: Optimization
The Search for the Subcontinents of the Mind
Development of Moment-by-Moment Measures
The Future: Seven Trends

II. Advertising Models 31
Television
Print

III. Report Card Measures From Different
Pre-Testing Systems .49
Introduction
Attention and Recall
Branding
Motivation and Persuasion
Composite Measures
Liking
Recognition vs. Recall: Tracking Advertising
   in the Marketplace

IV. Leading Audience Attention 75
Thin-Slicing Experience
Editing Film
Flow of Attention

V. Four Dramatic Structures of Emotional
TV Advertising 93
Flow of Emotion and Performance Measures
   on Pretests
Four Dramatic Structures
Four Different Roles of the Brand
Summary

VI. Film Tips For Branding TV Commercials . . .107
   Why is Brand Linkage Important?
   Film Tips to Enhance Brand Linkage

VII. Finding Ideas That Travel: What to Look
   For in Advertising Global Brands 125
   Creative Options
   Barriers to Universal Advertising
   Keys to International Advertising Effectiveness:
      What We Have Learned
   International Barriers to Executional
      Effectiveness

VIII. Five Research Strategies For Improving
   Advertising Productivity, *with John*
   Kastenholz 137
   1: Test the Advertising Creative With a
      Valid Performance Standard
   2: Rehearse the Creative in Rough Form
      First
   3: Experiment With Creative Alternatives
   4: Optimize the Creative With Diagnostic
      Insights
   5: Learn From the Competition

IX. How to Have a Successful Research Meeting
   With the Ad Team 153
   What Are the Barriers to Successful
      Collaboration?
   Group Interaction: Dialogue is the Heart of
      Group Learning
   The Roles in the Meeting: Understanding
      the Emotional Dynamics in the Room
   The Three Conditions Necessary for
      Discourse
   Causes of Failure and Success Factors in a
      Research Meeting

X. How To Talk the Talk: A Glossary of Advertising
   Research Terms 177

XI. **Resources** 231
    Websites
    Notes
    Publications
    Rough Guide to Statistical Testing

Foreword

A.G. Lafley, President and Chief Executive of The Procter & Gamble Company, recently stated that "the best brands win two crucial moments of truth. The first moment occurs at the store shelf, when a consumer decides whether to buy one brand over another. The second moment occurs at home, when he or she uses the brand and is delighted or isn't."

I think there is a third moment of truth for most brands. In many cases it occurs before the store shelf or in-home use experience. It happens when a message is sent by an advertiser and received by a consumer. Sometimes it is used to introduce us to new products, sometimes to communicate improvements to existing brands. At other times to show us how certain brands can make our lives better. But in all cases, consistently great advertising must stop us and capture our attention, create the proper brand linkage, inform us, move us emotionally, persuade us to buy and in the end leave a positive impression of the brand. The challenge for marketers is to find valid and reliable ways to measure these components of effective advertising.

This handbook is for everyone from the most experienced researchers, brand managers and creatives to those learning about advertising research for the first time. It provides a comprehensive review of key metrics used by major pre-testing systems along with a glossary of terms, tips for branding TV commercials as well as advice on how to have a successful research meeting. It provokes everyone to think harder about how advertising works.

In short, this handbook is for those who want to know their craft better, stimulate their thinking and compete better in the marketplace.

Michael Robinson,
DDB Worldwide Advertising

Introduction

For most people, a first-time visit to a new domain of knowledge is like a visit to a foreign country. The language is strange, the money is confusing, the proper names are peculiar, and while many things may look the same as they appear in their home country, the rules are subtly different. So different that, if a person is not careful, they may unexpectedly find themselves driving on the wrong side of the road.

In terms of relative size the domain of advertising research is like the very small Duchy of Grand Fenwick nestled somewhere between the much larger nations of Advertising and Finance, Hollywood and Business, Science and Art. Being at the crossroads of many disciplines, our small country attracts many tourists—account planners, brand managers, creative directors—though few are actual full time citizens as I am.

Much like a guide to Paris or Tokyo, I have written this book as a helpful guide for the tourist or occasional visitor who, upon passionately pursuing the dream of a powerful advertising campaign, finds him or herself stopped at a border checkpoint by one of our customs inspectors.

This book is intended to be neither a comprehensive nor an in-depth study of the subject. This is a reference piece. It's a survival guide to throw in your backpack and pull out now and then when needed as you trek through the forest of advertising research concepts and over the mountain passes of pre-test hurdle rates that you may encounter.

The book is divided into eleven chapters that represent distinct, but useful views of the landscape. The first three are strictly about research: the history, the theory, and the measurement practices of advertising research.

The next four chapters shift to a creative viewpoint. Sections four and five examine the structure of film from two very different psychological perspectives, cognition and affect. Chapter four looks at television commercials from the standpoint of film syntax, which pertains to how film is edited to control the flow of audience attention from the beginning to the end of the ad. Chapter five deals with dramatic structure, a discussion of the different ways that emotions can be deployed in the service of the brand. In chapter six there's a review of the many effective film techniques for branding commercials. And in chapter seven, there is an essay about the creative risks to avoid in developing multi-cultural, global ad campaigns.

Chapters eight and nine deal with research viewed as a business process. It's from a manager's perspective. Chapter eight identifies five strategies for using ad research effectively in the creative development process, and chapter nine provides guidelines on how to have a successful research meeting with your ad team.

Next, there's a concise glossary for the language of the locals.

And finally, there's an academic reference section at the end where you can read more deeply about the subjects only touched on here.

For clarity, let me expand just a bit.

In the opening we are taken on a brief guided tour of the history of pre-testing, looking back over the past fifty years of debate and development, from recall testing to measuring communication and persuasion, to the current focus on the problem of how to measure emotions in advertising. It briefly answers the question "How did we get here?" so that we can more clearly see how to move forward in our understanding of how to measure advertising effectiveness.

Next we will visit the major theoretical concepts of advertising pre-testing. Nearly all advertising researchers can agree that these constructs are important, though they may disagree about the relative importance of each. This chapter introduces a heuristic model— a "teaching model"—that provides the reader with an intuitive road map of how these different ideas are connected. A model, of course, is a bit like a Gothic cathedral that is always under construction, so this should only be viewed as a convenient place to start your tour and not the final destination.

The chapter on measurement—a summary of the key metrics used to "grade" advertising—is where we find the most disagreement among the leading research providers. Whether inches are better than centimeters, or, mixing constructs, how you translate miles into the number of Euros needed for the taxi ride, are analogs to the ideas that are debated among ad researchers. There are no final answers in this section, but you will learn what the arguments are. In the marketplace of research ideas, the buyer should beware.

In the following two chapters of the book television commercials are examined through the lens of the filmmaker. Hollywood has taught the world how to watch movies so that the visual language of film is a universal language. Clear, easy-to-follow film syntax operates in accordance with underlying psychological principles. The first of these two pieces discusses our research findings related to how, on a cognitive level, audiences watch movies. Similarly, dramatic structure is important for creating those emotional effects that turn mere products into brands that consumers love. The second describes four different dramatic structures that have been proven effective in emotional advertising.

For the ad professional the subject of branding is always playing in the theater of the mind. Context, continuity, close-up, cuts, and camera angles are among the filmmaking variables that have measurable consequences for the performance of a commercial execution in a pre-test. If you have a problem with a brand linkage score, this chapter provides an actionable checklist of things to talk about with your creative collaborators in the film editing room.

In a world of global brands multi-national corporations now import and export advertising executions as readily as products and services. Finding advertising ideas that travel well can be a major competitive advantage. Fortunately, storytelling is a universal art that advertisers can use to build a global brand, but pitfalls await the culturally insensitive. In the travel section we share some of the lessons we have learned from testing ideas across many borders.

While everyone understands the importance of having a good strategy for developing an effective advertising campaign, many overlook the importance of having clear strategies for learning. The opening piece on research viewed as a business process describes five strategies for deploying pre-testing research in the creative development process that have been proven effective by one of the largest, most successful consumer packaged goods companies in the world, Unilever.

Successful pre-testing research is research that actually gets used to make better advertising. The piece on how to have a successful research meeting with the ad team describes the different role that each of the players in the conference room can play in getting to a productive, positive learning experience, even if the research news is bad.

No one likes to feel like a Yokel on his first visit to New York—especially if you've come to attend your first presentation of ad research results—so the Glossary provides a handy dictionary for talking to the natives.

Finally, for additional reading there's a reference section of books and journal articles for a deeper dive on the subjects covered in this handbook. There is also a list of useful Websites. And, for the less mathematically minded reader, there is a tip sheet of statistical rules-of-thumb for analyzing those numbers-filled research reports.

Advertising research, like advertising itself, is a business of people and ideas. Hopefully, this handbook will give you a feel for the range of ideas that our people struggle with every day to make this a useful business for our clients and their advertising agencies. This work itself is the product of many minds and many hands. I'd like to give special thanks to the generous clients and my hardworking fellow citizens at CY Research who made it possible.

Charles Young
Albuquerque, 2005

The
Advertising Research
Handbook

I
A Short History of
Television Copytesting

1

A Short History of Television Copytesting

In the late 1950s and early 1960s, television was just over a decade into its commercialization stage, about as far as the Internet is today. In those days there were just three networks. Programming was in black and white. A modern television viewer just might find the content tedious in terms of its visual pacing, and heavy on dialogue compared to the sophisticated cinematography of today.

Television advertising was different then, too. The basic unit of advertising was longer—the 60-second commercial. Many brands advertised in sole sponsor shows without commercial clutter. And there were fewer brands doing television advertising—but with more commercials surrounding the brand with a variety of messages.

To illustrate the last point: some years ago, an advertising agency undertook a bit of advertising archaeology, reviewing the ancient history of two Proctor and Gamble (P & G) brands which they had handled from their very beginning. The agency was quite surprised to learn how much things had changed since the golden age of television. In 1959, P & G launched *Mr. Clean* household cleanser nationally and, during the first eighteen months of its introduction, aired 35 different sixty-second executions. In 1961, when P & G launched *Head & Shoulders* shampoo, 27 distinct executions ran during the first eighteen months. Today, either brand would be lucky to produce two to three commercials in a given year and one would probably be a :15.

The reason for this profligate rate of commercial production was quite simple. According to historical records tracked down in the 4A's library in New York, in 1960 an average network-quality sixty-second commercial would cost you $10,000 to produce— one-fortieth the cost of today's production. An A-list director would cost you around $3,500. A tiny fraction of today's fees. Not surprisingly, given the low cost of commercial production, doing research on creative effectiveness was considered a relatively simple and straightforward filtering process.

In the years since, however, various methods of research have been developed to manage the risk associated with increasingly expensive media budgets. This category of research has historically been known as copytesting or, more correctly, pre-testing. Implicitly, all of these methods are intended to be *predictive* of commercial performance in some way. The other major form of quantitative advertising research which also developed over this time period involves tracking the effects of television advertising once it has actually aired and separating those effects from other variables in the marketing mix, as exemplified by Millward Brown's continuous tracking service offering.[1, 2] This form of research is *explanatory* in nature, rather than predictive, and provides valid surrogate measures for the return on the advertising investment. It's an equally fascinating story, but beyond the scope of this work.

Much of the history of copytesting resembles the fable of the three blind men describing the elephant with recall or persuasion replacing snake or tree trunk as the competing descriptions of the advertising animal. So, not surprisingly, clients have been much confused by the various pictures painted by the different copytesting systems to describe how advertising works. Yet most of the widely-used approaches are probably valid up to a point. In the past twenty years, suppliers have produced an endless series of validation charts and regression lines with high r-squared statistics in support of their claim to having the best copytesting system. It should be noted that this wasn't always the case. As documented by Ostlund, Clancy, and Sapra, industry frustration with the lack of research hygiene among copytesting firms had reached a peak level shortly before the advent of the retail scanner revolution.[3]

So why do client and agency frustrations persist, despite the ongoing evolution and "scientification" of copytesting? This frustration comes from overpromise and oversimplification of a complex subject—the question of how an endless variety of television commercials penetrate the human mind to motivate everyday behavior. Really, when you think about it, rocket science looks easy by comparison.

Because the U.S. was the dominant market for television advertising during this period, the story of how television copytesting evolved in the U.S. essentially highlights the various management debates over this time about how advertising is supposed to work—an issue that still holds our attention today with the emergence of global advertising campaigns and the proliferation of media choices. The current time, therefore, is a good vantage point for reviewing where we have been in our thinking. What follows is an attempt to provide a broad overview of the subject so that researchers currently in the field can move forward.

There are four general themes woven into the last half-century of copytesting. The first is the quest for a valid single-number statistic to capture the overall performance of the advertising creative. This is an attempt to summarize the various report card measures which are used to *filter* commercial executions and help management make the go/no go decision about which ads to air. The second theme is the development of diagnostic copytesting, whose main purpose is *optimization*, providing insights about and understanding of a commercial's performance on the report card measures with the hope of identifying creative opportunities to save and improve executions. The third theme is the development of *non-verbal* measures in response to the belief of many advertising professionals that much of a commercial's effects—e.g., the emotional impact—may be difficult for respondents to put into words or scale on verbal rating statements and may, in fact, be operating below the level of consciousness. The fourth theme, which is a variation on the previous two, is the development of *moment-by-moment* measures to describe the internal dynamic structure of the viewer's experience of the commercial, as a diagnostic counterpoint to the various gestalt measures of commercial performance or predicted impact.

THE REPORT CARD MEASURES:
FILTERING THE CREATIVE

Regardless of the issues of inspiration, risk-taking and creative freedom that are involved in the conceptualization of advertising executions, from a management perspective the creative development process is an expensive business process which outputs products—i.e., commercials—of highly variable quality. Like any industrial process, control is a function of our ability to measure it. For large firms, those for which advertising is mission-critical to their business, such as P & G, significant quantities of advertising executions are produced every year. Therefore, very simple metrics are needed to provide senior managers with a clear picture of how well the process is working and to provide a check on the quality of the decisions being made by the more junior brand managers and agency teams who are charged with the day-to-day business of making advertising. The key problem, of course, is one of validity—the relationship to sales.

The logic behind the first report card measure for testing television ads, the Day After Recall (DAR) score, is quite simple. For advertising to be effective, it must surely leave some trace behind in the memory of the consumer. This memory effect metric was particularly credible given the traditional argument that advertising is superior to short-term promotions such as couponing only because of its long-term effect on sales. Recall testing, therefore, was interpreted to measure an ad's ability on air to break through into the mind of the consumer to register a message from the brand in long-term memory.

According to Honomichl, DAR testing was first applied to the advertising measurement problem by George Gallup Sr., who built on R & D work done by a Naval Commander named Thompson who used it in the training of Navy pilots during the Second World War.[4] The Compton advertising agency then took up the development of the measure, evaluating an arbitrary range of forgetting periods such as 12, 24, 48 and 72 hours and exploring a range of variables operating in the on-air viewing environment. Compton soon began promoting it to their clients as proof of performance for their work. P & G conducted experiments of its own, became convinced of the usefulness of the measure, and subcontracted the fieldwork to a then small research company in Cincinnati called Burke. With P & G taking the lead, many other advertisers soon followed suit and Burke DAR testing became the dominant copytesting report card measure for the fifties and sixties.

In the seventies, however, some researchers began to question the relationship between recall and sales. According to some reports at the time, P & G reviewed a hundred split-cable test markets that had been conducted over ten years with ads that had been recall-tested and had been unable to find a significant relationship between recall scores and sales response. Not coincidentally, in a major validation study conducted at roughly the same time, Ross found that persuasion was a better predictor of sales response to advertising than was recall.[5] Much later, Lodish and his colleagues conducted an even more extensive review of test market results and also failed to find a relationship between recall and sales.[6]

During this period, therefore, the attention of advertising researchers shifted to the problem of measuring advertising persuasiveness. One of the researchers leading the way was Horace Schwerin, who pointed out "...the obvious truth is that a claim can be well remembered but completely unimportant to the prospective buyer of the product—the solution the marketer offers is addressed to the wrong need."[7] Schwerin sold his company (and the pre-post shift approach to measuring persuasion that he developed) to ARS, which succeeded in getting it adopted by P & G as the new standard for measuring advertising effectiveness.

Recall continued to be provided as a companion measure, in part to ease the transition for the old-line researchers, with the caveat that recall is important up to some minimal threshold level, but persuasion is the more important measure. Again, with the imprimatur of P & G support, the ARS pre-post measure of persuasiveness became the category leader for much of the seventies and eighties.[8] Alternative post-exposure measures of motivation or persuasiveness were also developed at this time such as the weighted five-point purchase intent scale—the industry gold standard for concept testing (which is currently used by the BASES simulated test market system as well as by several copytesting companies).

Meanwhile, other researchers during the late seventies began to question the validity of recall as a measure of breakthrough.[9] To some researchers, the construct of breakthrough is about the ability of the commercial execution to win the fight for attention and get noticed immediately, which is what many Creatives assume is the first task that advertising must perform in creating a sale. Of course, this is not the same as measuring what happens to a commercial after it's been processed through long-term memory. An important distinction was made between the attention-getting power of the creative execution and how well branded the ad was. One of the reasons an ad may fail in a recall test, it was argued, even if it broke through the clutter and garnered a lot of attention, is that the memory of it might simply be filed away improperly in the messy filing cabinets of the mind so that it becomes difficult to retrieve with the standard verbal recall prompts.

This debate ran parallel to the ongoing debate of recall versus recognition as the best approach for tracking advertising awareness in market.

These two very different ways of tapping into memory for evidence of advertising awareness can produce very different measurements, usually substantially higher for recognition.[10]

For researchers on the recall side of the debate, the standard approach to measuring ad recall with telephone surveys provides consistency and comparability between the recall results of a pre-test and those of a post-test. Those on the recognition side of the debate remind us that memory is a complex subject, and that more than one memory system of the mind may be involved in determining advertising effectiveness.

Consider the difference between one's failure to recall the name yet ability to recognize the face of someone one has met before. For most people, the fact that one can recognize a face is taken as the more reliable "proof" that one has actually met a person before. In the last few years, the Internet has now created a practical research opportunity, unavailable in telephone surveys, to show consumers the "face" of an ad—i.e., a film clip or storyboard—in order to measure ad awareness with recognition-based questions.

Several companies, such as MSW Research, DRI, and Ameritest have developed alternative pre-testing approaches to recall testing as a measure of commercial breakthrough.[11] In these systems, attention and branding are measured separately. These approaches involve simulating a cluttered media environment off-air and measuring which ads win the fight for attention without the intervening variable of a day's worth of forgetting time. Recent research, jointly published by Unilever and Ameritest, has added substance to the debate by showing the findings from an analysis of a large database of commercials that had been tested with both approaches.[12] These results show that recall scores and attention scores are completely uncorrelated, suggesting that these two approaches to measuring breakthrough are in fact measuring completely different things. Moreover, recall scores for this set of ads had a strong negative correlation with commercial likability ratings, confirming what creative directors have been telling researchers about recall tests for many years.

Different approaches were also developed during this period to measure the well-brand-edness of a commercial. Ipsos-ASI views brand linkage as the missing variable between recall and recognition and computes a measure of brandedness by looking at the ratio of a com-mercial's recall score to its recognition score (derived by reading a verbal description of an ad to the respondent). The Millward Brown approach to branding uses a five-point rating scale to measure how well a commercial execution is custom tailored to "fit" the brand.

A third approach, used by Ameritest, measures branding by tracking a respondent's top-of-mind propensity to use the brand name as the "handle" to retrieve the memory of an advertising execution immediately after exposure in a cluttered media environment. Unfortunately, by using the same branding label to name three different measurement constructs, ad researchers continue to add to the confusion surrounding report card measures. Unilever just reported an analysis of a database of commercials triple-tested with all three types of measures, showing that each of the three is measuring something uncorrelated with, and therefore different from, the other two.[13]

Finally, a very different approach was used by Millward Brown to create report card measures of commercial performance. In the late eighties, working with Unilever, they used a modeling approach to derive an overall effectiveness index from various component measures. Instead of starting with an *a priori* theoretical model of how the mind is supposed to interact with advertising, they reverse engineered the process by running a massive stepwise regression to identify pre-testing measures predictive of advertising tracking results (from their continuous tracking program) and then used a black box approach to combine these component measures into an overall predictive score. While not directly validated by sales, this approach had the appeal of creating consistency between the two approaches (pre-testing and in-market tracking) that a company like Unilever uses to grade advertising performance.

Over the last fifty years, category leadership in terms of market share for the commercial firms providing copytesting services has turned on the measure currently in vogue as the magic number predicting in-market performance. First, it was Burke's DAR score. Then it was ARS's measure of persuasion benchmarked against fair share. Currently in the U.S., it is Ipsos-ASI's copy effect score, a composite measure integrating recall and persuasion. And, coming on strong in this highly competitive market, we have Millward Brown, the category leader outside the U.S., with its effectiveness index.

THE ROLE OF DIAGNOSTICS: OPTIMIZATION

Accountability is always a tricky problem when it comes to marketing activities, since the real world where professionals operate has always been an exceedingly messy multivariate place in which to perform research. The mere fact that brands exist in the world is proof that marketing works at a general level. However, determining whether marketing resources have been allocated efficiently and effectively has always been a problem.

For that reason, providing marketers with

improvements that result in an incremental sense of control over even part of the complex marketing process will be rewarded generously by the marketplace. One of the biggest innovations in market research over the past half century has been the availability of retail scanner data. According to Moult, before the eighties, the average marketing budget was divided so that 43 percent of every marketing dollar was spent on advertising, while 57 percent was spent on consumer and trade promotion.[14] By the early nineties, advertising's share of the marketing dollar had shrunk to only 25 percent, and promotion had grown to 75 percent. What had changed, in the meantime, was a shift in the balance of accountability. With huge amounts of accurate retail sales data coming out of stores, it became easy to measure the short-term return on promotion while the effect of the advertising spending in the longer term became relatively less predictable and therefore riskier to use.

The desire to harness the creative power of advertising more effectively so as to attract those vanished client dollars has motivated the industry to embrace advertising tracking studies—witness the continuous tracking and marketing mix modeling services offered by Millward Brown—to justify advertising budgets. This put a spotlight back on the renewed need for pre-testing measurements to predict the performance of advertising prior to airing.

But meeting the client's need for account-ability has long been a source of conflict within advertising agencies. In particular, most Creatives are skeptical of the value of copytesting. It is common for Creative Directors to caution us of the dangers inherent in "writing to the test," where advertising is created based on a formula for what tests well rather than truly original work that re-defines a market-place. They express concern, also, at the in-efficiency of throwing away good creative ideas that are designed to operate differently than the researchers' models imply—the role of emotion in advertising is an example of the debates which arise from this longstanding issue. From an agency perspective, pre-testing research provides value only if it delivers an understanding of why a commercial scores the way it does and insights into how to improve an ad's performance—how to clean and polish the creative idea to a shining brightness.

One of the earliest agencies to embrace diagnostic copytesting was Leo Burnett. In the sixties, ad researchers Bill Wells and Clark Leavitt, and, later on, Fred and Mary Jane Schlinger developed a diagnostic pre-test for the agency called Communication Workshop.[15, 16] Extensive attitudinal rating statements were developed and factor-analyzed to provide a multidimensional profile of how a commercial was working in dimensions such as relevant news, believability, entertainment value and uniqueness. In addition, a series of open-ended questions were developed (based on the classic qualitative research funnel from general to specific) to provide insight into respondent reactions and message takeaway from the execution. A great deal of effort was also invested in developing complex coding schemes to better understand respondent reactions. For example, coding for product/narrative integration became a key source of insight into the well-brandedness of executions. The general way this form of research was positioned within the agency can be found in the policy that was upheld for many years that the research be conducted at agency expense and results be shared with Creatives for learnings, and shown to clients *only with the Creative Director's permission*. The test was designed only to be a tool for learning and optimization, not to be a report card.

Following Burnett's lead, many other agencies developed their own custom approaches to testing their own work. Key to the agency approach to copytesting is the belief that advertising operates in more than one way and that the methods that are effective in reaching consumers at one point in time may become less relevant as the consumer becomes vaccinated against various styles of advertising. This makes agencies suspicious of report card measures since the lessons from such systems always seem to point to one particular type of advertising approach. For example, "show the brand early and often" is advice often given by copytest systems based on DAR. Agencies also typically question the validity of a one-number approach to capture the complex workings of an ad.

Agency research departments were downsized in the eighties as a result of advertising's shrinking share of the marketing dollar and client price resistance to media inflation and consequent pressure on agency margins. Since that time, most agencies have gotten out of the business of testing their own ads. To most clients, this smacked too much of the fox watching the henhouse, anyway. Nevertheless, agencies tended to push hard for softer, more qualitative approaches to understanding their work early in the creative development process and to opt for focus groups rather than quantitative research as a mechanism for injecting the voice of the consumer into the creative development process.

According to the 4A's, the cost of commercial production doubled during the 1990's, with the average cost to produce a network quality television commercial rising from $180,000 in 1989 to $358,000 in 2002 (see www.aaaa.org). This was twice the rate of inflation over the same period. At the same time, network audiences were shrinking. These factors all contributed to raising the risks associated with creating a television commercial but also shifted the interest of ad managers away from pure report-card testing systems like ARS and Ipsos-ASI and toward the hybrid systems combining validated performance measures with powerful diagnostics, systems like Millward Brown and Ameritest. The new need of the nineties was to squeeze every dollar's worth out of this increasingly expensive advertising film.

This shifted the value equation for the category away from simply filtering creative ideas on the basis of one report card measure or another, and put emphasis on gaining insights to improve the performance of individual executions. For some companies adopting this approach, the payback on research dollars has been considerable. In a recent review of the pretesting work done by Ameritest over the course of a year by one of the major divisions of Unilever, it was found that roughly forty percent

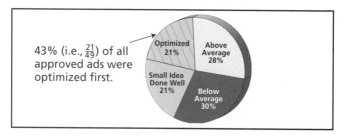

The new value proposition is filtering plus optimization.

of all ads approved for airing had been revised or re-edited based on insights provided by quantitative diagnostic research.

Among copytesting suppliers, most diagnostic copytesting tended to follow the lead set by the ad agencies with some version of a test consisting of open-ended questions and attitudinal rating statements that bears more than a superficial resemblance to the Burnett model. But, for many practitioners, this purely verbal approach to describing the communication and response to advertising messaging seemed to leave important aspects of an ad's performance out of the picture. A clue to the limitations of the current research paradigm could be seen in the category descriptor: why call it *copy*testing when it's for tele*vision*?

THE SEARCH FOR THE SUBCONTINENTS
OF THE MIND

It has long been a belief of advertising professionals that much of the way advertising works operates below the surface. Not that we believe in the subliminal advertising techniques popularized by Vance Packard's 1957 best seller *The Hidden Persuaders*. Nor do we believe in advertising magic. But our own day-to-day experience is that much of the way that we interpret the world is subtext; the mind is continuously engaged in the search for deeper meaning, understanding the important gaps between what we say and what we do.

The old proverb that "a picture is worth a thousand words" is completely untrue. There is information in every picture that we cannot put into words. There is something in the lovely sounds of our favorite music that we cannot verbalize—yet it moves us much more strongly than the literal meaning of the lyrics. This is the aesthetic information content of a television commercial. And the belief held by many advertising professionals is that traditional word-based research techniques—those protocols of open-ended questioning or ratings of semantic descriptions of the ad—somehow shortchange the best work.

For that reason, (and throughout the history of copytesting), there has been an interest in a range of nonverbal or physiological measures of advertising response. During the seventies, for example, Krugman published research on brain wave activity involved in viewing commercials.[17] Other researchers experimented with galvanic skin response, voice pitch analysis and eye-tracking methodology—all non-conscious measures of a biologic response that re-searchers tried to correlate with commercial performance. Many of these early efforts met with disappointing results, usually because of the limitations of the technology that was used at the time. Recently, there has been a resurgence of interest in these types of measures, such as using MRI scanners to visualize brain activity during the commercial viewing experience.[18]

A different approach to probing response to advertising film was developed by Ameritest in the nineties. The Ameritest Picture Sorts is a method of deconstructing a viewer's dynamic response to the film on multiple levels. The Flow of Attention, for example, measures how the eye pre-consciously filters the visual information in an ad and serves both as a gatekeeper for human consciousness and as an interactive search engine involved in the process of constructing perceptions of the brand. The focus of analysis is on understanding the role of film structure and syntax in creating those powerful film experiences that can provide the basis for the consumer's emotional relationship with the brand. An example of a Flow of Attention for one particular ad is shown below.

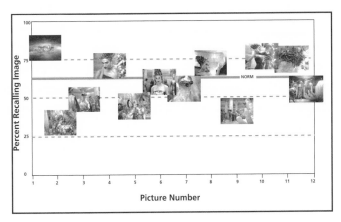

The Flow of Attention

More mainstream than the biological measures, the Picture Sorts has been used around the world by major advertisers as diverse as IBM and Unilever in their standard pre-testing process. The strength of the diagnostic relationship between the different "flow" measures and all the major report card measures produced by other pre-testing systems has been validated in a series of publications in the last few years.[19-24]

DEVELOPMENT OF MOMENT-BY-MOMENT MEASURES

One of the essential aspects of watching a television commercial is that it is a *temporal* experience—it's an unfolding of a sequence of ideas and emotions that takes place over time, in thirty seconds, or perhaps fifteen. From this research perspective, watching a television commercial is an event. Understanding the internal structure of that viewing event requires a very different approach to measurement.

The shift in analytic perspective from thinking of a commercial as the fundamental unit of measurement, a holistic and unified esthetic experience, to be rated in its entirety, to thinking of it in terms as a structured *flow* of experience gave rise to experimentation with moment-by-moment systems in the early eighties. As an analogy, this transition in thinking is similar in some respects to the ways in which quantum physicists struggled to define the nature of light: is it a particle or is it a wave? Effectiveness measures such as recall or persuasion take a *particle* view of advertising; the moment-by-moment diagnostics implied a *wave* view of the advertising experience. And like the theoretical resolution of modern physics, advertising researchers are now beginning to acknowledge the fundamentally *dual* nature of advertising.

In the 1980s, a number of firms commercialized moment-by-moment dial-a-meter response to television commercials. Viewfacts, MSW and Millward Brown used a trace methodology to produce a one-dimensional response function based on liking or interest. While relatively little has been published to validate the relationships between these dial-a-meter systems and the general report card measures of attention, branding, or motivation, anecdotal evidence suggests this diagnostic technique can be a useful tool in the hands of a skilled interpreter.

A more recent development of the past few years has been the Ameritest Picture Sorts® technique.

A key philosophical difference between the Picture Sorts and meter ratings approach is that, with the Picture Sorts, quantitative measurement is a function of the rate of information flow (or visual complexity) of an ad, whereas dial-a-meter approaches are based on mechanical clock time. The Picture Sorts approach shifts the frame of measurement to the flow of subjective time in the viewer's experience of the advertising. In addition, measurement is made in three dimensions, not one; the Flow of Attention, which measures how the parts of the ad are processed on a cognitive level; the Flow of Emotion, which measures how the emotions being produced by the ad can be processed in four different ways (shown below) to achieve different dramatic effects; and the Flow of Meaning, which quantifies how the emotions created by the ad are harnessed to illuminate a brand's core values—what we call the "working emotion" in an ad. The latter type of emotion is also what Aristotle called "aesthetic emotion," or emotion that carries with it a powerful meaning into the mind of the consumer.

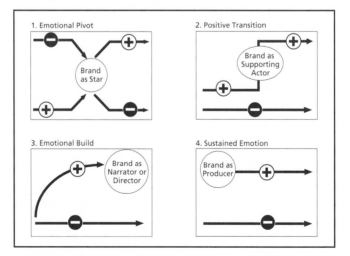

Ameritest has identified four different dramatic structures for effective emotional advertising.

The Future: Seven Trends

The state-of-the-art, circa the beginning of the twenty-first century, has been described. Looking backward for the past fifty years, we see that the art and science of measuring advertising has undergone a considerable amount of debate and change in our thinking and in our business practices. Looking around at the forces of change operating in our world today, there is no reason to think that the rate of change will slow down. The following are seven trends that will be shaping the way we do business in the future.

1. The emergence of global research standards for advertising global brands.

Increasingly, multi-nationals are focusing on the need to build global brands, and for their brands to speak with one voice around the world. This calls for global advertising campaigns that will be increasingly visual in style. Deploying global research systems to provide a standard way to measure advertising performance from one region to another, and for providing tools for making transparent how different cultural factors affect advertising response, will become an important management focus for managing ad spending in the global marketplace.

2. There will be more advertising measurement, not less.

Advertising is becoming more expensive and the range of executional options have become so diverse that more control over the process is being demanded by major clients today. Procurement departments, in particular, under the banner of accountability, are challenging advertising agencies and research companies to provide more proof of value to justify ad budgets. This will drive growth in this important sector of advertising research.

3. Most copytesting will move on to the Internet.

In an age of rapid-response marketing, the emphasis is on speed of decision-making. The Internet is the obvious choice for shortening the time involved in the research step of the creative development cycle. Many suppliers have already begun migrating their advertising research online (for both television and print testing). Economic pressure will probably force the majority of testing online in the near future.

4. The new value proposition will be filtering plus optimization.

For the foreseeable future, the cost of advertising executions will continue to go up. To manage that cost, managers will be increasingly concerned to make sure not only that they air their strongest ideas, but that they don't spend half their advertising budgets on *average* ideas. Ad managers will be looking for every opportunity to make executions work harder and research systems will outperform this growing category if they can *validate the power of their diagnostics*, providing proof that they actually help make ads more effective.

5. Ad research will move beyond semantics, putting a new emphasis on non-verbal measurement.

Both the forces of globalization and the evolution of rich, multi-sensory media environments will continue to challenge researchers to think beyond the boundaries of language and semantics in understanding how advertising builds brand image. Leading ad researchers of today, such as Gerald Zaltman of Harvard University[24], have pointed out that new learnings from neuroscientists over the last few years have challenged us to develop new methods and approaches to understanding the hidden responses of the mind.

6. New heuristic models will be built to help managers make ad decisions in a world increasingly confused by media fragmentation.

As the world of media becomes increasingly fragmented and media choices proliferate, the need for research is to *simplify* the decision-making process for advertising managers. This calls for new *heuristics* that describe how different media work, e.g., television versus print. These heuristics are necessary to provide a common measurement framework so that advertising managers trying to allocate budgets across television or print or the Internet can compare the relative strengths of the television executions to the print execution to the Internet ad.

7. New mathematical approaches will be developed to model advertising effects.

Currently, researchers working in the field of complexity and chaos theory have been revolutionizing approaches to studying complex, messy problems such as the seemingly random behavior of financial markets or the complex flows of industrial supply chains. A world center for this activity, the Santa Fe Institute in New Mexico, provides numerous examples of new dynamic, non-linear approaches to building computer models that move well beyond the predictive power of the traditional linear approach of regression modeling. (See www.santafe.edu) Up to now, few efforts have been made by advertising researchers to apply these mathematical techniques to advertising measurement—the very definition of a non-linear problem. But it's only a matter of time.

II
Advertising Models

II
Advertising Models

Television

A wise old researcher once explained that a market researcher has two jobs: first, to learn something useful that your clients didn't know before; and second, to teach them what you found out. Over time, researchers learn that the second job is the harder of the two. It is also the more important because it is the key to making sure that the research you do actually gets used.

This is particularly true of advertising pre-testing. No form of research is more fraught with barriers to learning. The issues raised by testing generate high anxiety for everyone around the conference room table having a vested interest in the advertising.

Confusion and anxiety do not, as a rule, form an ideal emotional climate for the learning process. Clarity and calmness are required.

How do we move beyond these limitations and become the teachers our clients need us to be? We must begin with a shared mental model.

To borrow from Peter Senge's well-known book on learning organizations, *The Fifth*

Discipline: "The effectiveness of a leader is related to the continual improvement of the leader's mental models." In other words, the decisions your clients make based on pre-testing research are as much a function of the mental models they have about how advertising works as they are of the information that you provide them.

The next time you are in a meeting where a new piece of advertising is being discussed, sit back and ask yourself, "How much of this discussion is actually about the particular ad under consideration, and how much of this is a debate about how advertising works in general?" Much of the discussion will probably be about the various mental models everyone has about advertising. That's a barrier to learning and effective decision making.

Different Mental Models of Advertising

First, let's remember *why* so many professionals have different mental models of advertising.

Dating back to the early days of television, the first widely used pre-testing measure was Burke's Day After *Recall* Score. This model held that the key to effectiveness is that an ad should leave some kind of trace in the memory of the consumer.

Unfortunately, after many years of empirically trying to correlate recall scores with sales results, a number of advertisers, such as

Proctor and Gamble, concluded that recall was missing something important. So, researchers searched for something else to predict sales. In the seventies, pre-testing research shifted its focus to measuring *motivation*, such as the Advertising Research Systems Corporation's (ARS) measure of persuasion.

In the eighties, another pre-testing company, ASI, found that recall could be better understood when its two component variables were separated: the *attention-getting* power of the commercial execution and the *linkage between the brand* and the commercial.

Meanwhile, other researchers argued that how well a commercial was liked was key—a result empirically confirmed by a famous advertising research foundation validity study.

Most researchers also agreed that *communication* of a strategic selling proposition was the key to effective advertising, a point of view that continues to sell a great many focus groups to this day.

Creatives, who appear to have different mental models of advertising than Researchers, have always intuitively felt that the *entertainment* value of a television commercial is paramount; that it's important to be fresh and different in order to stand apart from the crowd.

What about *emotion*? Emotion sells. Advertising agencies, like the Leo Burnett agency, developed complex methods of coding and analyzing the verbatims from open-ended questions and constructed batteries of diagnostic ratings statements to profile viewer response to commercials on multiple dimensions of both rational and emotional response.

And finally, a number of researchers believe that pre-testing shouldn't just be *copy*-testing, which is what this type of research has historically been called. After all, we are attempting to describe the consumer's tele-*vision* experience. These researchers experiment with *non-verbal* techniques: brain waves, skin galvanic response, voice pitch analysis, and picture sorts.

So the debate goes on to this day. No wonder Clients are confused and Creatives are skeptical!

A Model for Television Advertising Pre-Testing

Is the real question, "Which of the above measurements is the correct one?" Consider this: many smart people have been working on this problem for years and each theory is probably right to some degree. From a learning standpoint, the real problem may be one of synthesis and interpretation.

If the goal is to make smarter decisions about advertising, so that the brand will become a leader in its business category, then ask yourself, "How do I fit these different ways of measuring the advertising experience together into a more *complete* and *intuitive* description of the advertising?"

Our answer to this question is the following advertising model.

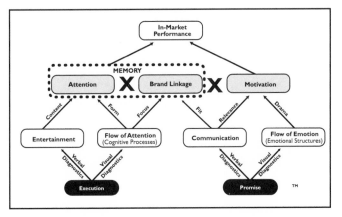

Ameritest's Heuristic Television Advertising Model

This is a *heuristic* model or teaching model. The purpose of the model is to focus attention on learning *how* and *why* an ad is working, with the goal of improving understanding and aiding judgement. The model organizes all the questions asked by earlier theories in order to provide us with a complete picture of how to fit together all the different dimensions of performance that modern ad researchers usually attempt to measure.

In the model, information is arranged in a hierarchy that bridges the divide of report card systems provided by some ad researchers and the diagnostic systems provided by others.

At the top is what pre-testing is supposed to predict: in-market results.

One level down are the *evaluative* measures that provide the "report card" portion of the research. These are the measures that are used to make the go/no go decision. Taken together, they answer the question, "Is this advertising good enough to put on air?"

Two levels down are the "diagnostic" measures that are correlated with, and therefore *explain*, the evaluative measures above. These are the measures that can be used to optimize the advertising. They answer the question, "How could I improve this ad?"

The arrows in the model highlight the primary relationships between the different variables measured. This is a road map for interpreting the data.

Essentially, the model says that for any commercial to be effective it must accomplish three things:

1. It must get noticed and attract an audience.

2. The audience must know who is sending the advertising message.

3. Once the commercial has the audience's attention; it must "sell" them something—i.e., motivate sales in the short run or at least create a positive predisposition for sales in the long run.

Evaluative variables are at the top of the heuristic ad model.

Other variables are important only insofar as they help to explain the variables of Attention, Brand Linkage and Motivation. For example, entertainment value or the originality of the execution is not important in and of itself but because it is an important predictor of Attention.

The same is true of liking. On the face of it, it may be possible for a commercial to not be well liked and still be effective. Wisk's "Ring Around the Collar" campaign is a widely mentioned example. Getting into the conscious mind of the consumer and selling the brand is always the bottom line for advertising!

Diagnostics

The model shows us that Attention is a function of two primary aspects of the execution:

1. Entertainment: Does the execution entertain or reward viewers with an enjoyable or engaging and unique experience in return for the 15 or 30 seconds that they are asked to spend with your client's message?

2. Flow of Attention: Is the execution a well-edited piece of film in terms of structure and syntax that captures and maintains the viewer's attention over time, focusing their thoughts and feelings on the important ideas and images in the commercial at a pace they can easily keep up with?

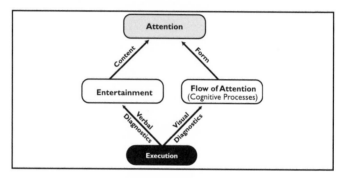

The Attention component of the heuristic model is about the form and content.

Branding is a function of two other constructs:
1. Focus: At some point in the film does the

The Brand Linkage component of the heuristic model is about focus and fit.

execution focus your attention on the brand being advertised?

2. Fit: How well does the execution fit the perception of the brand that the consumer already has?

Motivation is also a function of two separate constructs:

1. Communication: How relevant, believable and brand differentiating is the strategic promise you are communicating to your customer?

2. Flow of Emotion: How much emotion have you tapped into with the power of film to make your brand's promise seem "larger than life" and even more compelling?

In short, the key to Motivation is communicating a relevant idea in a dramatic way.

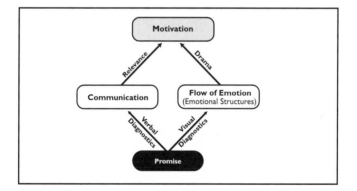

The Motivation component of the heuristic model is about relevance and drama.

Print

While there are no formulas for effective advertising, there are general principles that need to be taken into account when trying to penetrate the mind with effective selling ideas.

It's important not to think of print ads as static simply because they don't have temporal dimensions like TV commercials. Although a print ad doesn't move, the consumer's mind must move through the ad to create an effective advertising experience. Researchers need to help our clients think of print in a more dynamic way.

Just as with television advertising, remember that the human eye is not a camera, or a passive recorder of stimuli. Instead, think of the eye as an intelligent search engine, an active gate-keeper for the mind. Over half the human brain is devoted to creating what we call *visual perception*. That is why a measurement of what the eye sees is an incomplete understanding of what the conscious mind of the reader *constructs* from the images and ideas in the ad. So, from a diagnostic standpoint, you need a dynamic way of measuring how the mind is processing an advertisement.

Metaphors help us think clearly about complex subjects. A useful metaphor is to think of a print ad as kind of a virtual store, where the consumer is "shopping information."

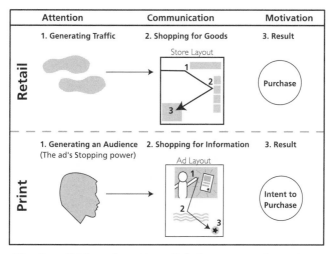

The Retail Metaphor: Parallels between print advertising and the retail in-store environment.

If you were the manager of a store, there would be three things you would try to do to build your business:

1. Get customers through the door by using attention-getting devices to generate traffic to the store;

2. Plan the layout of your store very carefully so customers can find what they are looking for and discover something while browsing;

3. Make sure you have closed the sale and motivate them to buy something before leaving.

These same general principles apply when you analyze a print ad. Ask yourself:

1. Is there a clear entry point to the ad where the majority of readers start their journey?

2. Is the path through the ideas and images

clear and easy to follow in a continuous sequence so the reader has a cohesive advertising experience?

3. Does the reader have a selling idea or brand image in their mental shopping basket before they get to your brand "checkout counter," i.e., your logo?

Print is a more active medium than TV in the sense that more work is required from the audience in processing the information in the ad. Because of this potentially higher level of involvement from readers of print ads, it is possible to transmit more complex messages in a print ad than a TV ad. However, we also know that readers are quite frugal with the time they will spend with advertising messages.

A Model for Print Advertising Pre-Testing

Importantly, most of what we need to measure about print advertising is very similar to what needs to be measured for a TV commercial. Attention-getting power is important for both kinds of advertising. Both print and TV ads need to be well branded to be effective. And both must motivate a sale. Indeed, we only need to change one variable in our TV model to have a model for print—the cognitive measure of the Flow of Attention.

However, television and print are different in two important ways: First, the order in which readers process the ideas and images and second, the amount of time readers spend with the ad is under the control of the audience for print, but not for TV. For example, one reader may start with the headline, while another starts with the main visual. And one reader may spend ten seconds looking at the ad, while another flips the page after a half second glance. To reflect these differences between the two mediums, the print model needs a different measurement of Flow of Attention, and a measure of "stickiness" which tells us how much time the reader would spend with the ad in the real world environment.

For print, the construct of Flow of Attention introduces "time into space"; the inverse operation of the technique used in TV which "freezes time" so that we can study the level of audience attention at different moments in the ad.

From an integrated marketing standpoint, the use of a similar model for TV and print leads to

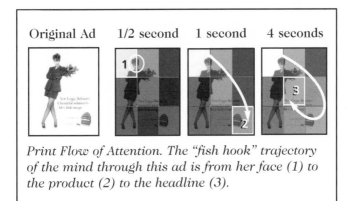

Print Flow of Attention. The "fish hook" trajectory of the mind through this ad is from her face (1) to the product (2) to the headline (3).

considerable efficiencies. By using a common measurement framework, you can compare TV test results with print test results in the same report. And more importantly, integrated models provide a simple and coherent way to think about and manage those seemingly different modes of communication in an increasingly fragmented world of media choices.

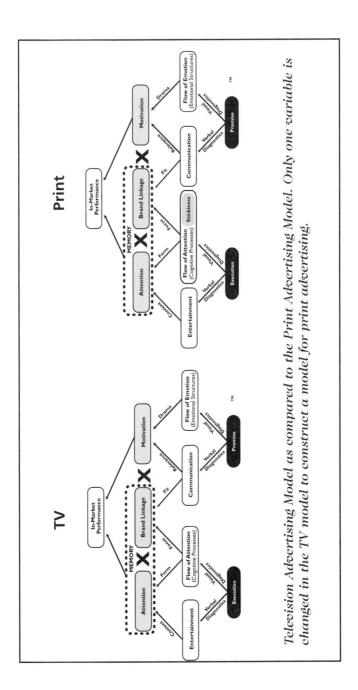

Television Advertising Model as compared to the Print Advertising Model. Only one variable is changed in the TV model to construct a model for print advertising.

III

Report Card Measures From Different Pre-Testing Systems

III

Report Card Measures From Different Pre-Testing Systems

INTRODUCTION

While most of the major research providers today agree that attention-getting power, branding, and motivation are all critical components of advertising effectiveness, each approaches the problem of how to measure these theoretical constructs somewhat differently.

In this chapter we will provide an overview of the various methods used to measure each of these constructs. We have attempted to summarize the major differences between methods. At the end of this book we also provide a list of journal articles providing quantitative evidence in support of the various arguments different suppliers make in favor of each of the different approaches. While we have a preference for our own approach, we also believe that other approaches have merit and may represent a piece of the total "truth" of advertising. Consequently, we have attempted to be as fair as possible in our description of the objective differences between systems.

We cannot, of course, describe every pre-testing system available in the market since there are so many. Those reviewed here were selected because they represent the leaders in the industry, and together account for perhaps as much as 70% of the television pretesting category.

Unfortunately, while the medium is older, the theory of testing print advertising is much more fragmented and less well-developed. Unlike television, there is no dominant approach to testing print, though various approaches to eye-tracking—Perception Research offline, or the Ameritest online approach—are among the most favored. For that reason we have chosen to omit a review of the print testing systems and instead simply focus on television.

Advertising research is a continually evolving business, particularly during this period when everyone is attempting to adjust their methods to the new reality of the internet. Moreover, as the other research suppliers we reference here are our competitors, we may simply not be aware of the latest developments in their systems. We assume, therefore, that as poten-tial buyers of pre-testing research, anyone reading this book would do their home-work in contacting these companies for additional details and updates.

We leave the conclusion to the reader as to

which is the best approach to measuring each dimension of advertising performance.

ATTENTION AND RECALL

Most pre-testing systems report some kind of measure of "breakthrough," either recall or attention, as an indicator of how efficiently a commercial execution will leverage a given level of media weight to capture a wide audience for the advertiser's message.

Even though they are both considered measures of breakthrough by users of the different systems, published research confirms that recall and attention measure fundamentally different aspects of commercial performance. Our own research suggests that recall is a measure of teaching—how effective a commercial is if you simply view it as a sales presentation of product information or product "news." Attention, even when measured in a variety of different ways, is a better measure of intrusiveness or breakthrough, rewarding executions that are interesting, involving, and unique—critical dimensions of performance in this new age of permission-based marketing.

Undoubtedly, recall is an appropriate measure for certain advertising applications. However, it appears to reward only one kind of advertising; ads where the brand is cued early and often and the focus is on communicating rational product features and benefits—i.e., ads that have a linear, rational structure.

Our experience is that advertising can work in more than one way and some of these other ways may be more appropriate when you are attempting to differentiate your brand based on emotional, rather than rational, consumer benefits.

Moreover, the various systems measure even the same constructs differently. In measuring recall, for example, different systems employ different periods of forgetting time: the original Burke, and later, the Ipsos-ASI systems give the consumer 24 hours to forget the advertising before calling them back, while ARS allows 72 hours of forgetting time. The original Burke system exposed the test ad "on air" to obtain results as close to the real world as possible, while for a variety of reasons Ipsos-ASI mails respondents a videotape which they can watch at home. ARS exposes ads in a theater setting with a large group of respondents at a time. These kinds of practical differences can affect the direct comparability of measures from different systems even if they all claim to be measuring recall.

One of the main philosophical differences between systems is whether or not the test ad should be embedded in a program environment so that the ad has to compete for attention against other advertising during breaks within a simulated television show.

The chief argument in favor of this approach

is that context affects communication, and by
simulating the programming context the test is
more like the real world. Interestingly, the
argument against is also that context is such a
powerful and unpredictable variable that we
should be cautious about introducing it into the
measurement. A given commercial may be
strongly helped by appearing in the context of
a comedy show, while it may by penalized by
appearing in the context of a drama. Another
commercial may do well in a drama, but not in
a comedy. By not simulating all possible
programming effects in some randomized
order, systems that use program environments
run the risk of introducing a bias into the measurement that affects the test ad in an unpredictable way, favoring some while penalizing
others. Since a pre-test should be a test of the
strength of the creative idea and not the media
buy, some testing systems prefer taking the
standard scientific approach of controlling or
eliminating those variables that are not the
subject of the measurement.

Another important difference between testing systems is the size of the database of norms
that would be available for interpreting test
results. Most clients would agree that the most
relevant benchmarks for a test ad would be
those that are "closest" to the work—either
the client's own most recent advertising that
has been successful in the marketplace or,

perhaps, the current advertising campaign that the competition is running. Norms, however, provide a useful frame of reference for interpreting "how high is up," putting the test data in the context of the best and worst advertising that has been tested over the years.

Most systems will provide norms according to the characteristics of the test execution—for example, providing different norms (and clutter reels) for animatics than for finished film. Commercial length (e.g., :15 vs. :30 vs. :60) is a variable that also appears to affect both recall and attention scores in most—but not all—systems. Typically the longer, and therefore more expensive formats, are rewarded with higher breakthrough scores.

Obviously, the older the system, the larger the norm base will be. However, the emergence of the internet as a primary channel of data collection changes the game somewhat, since on-line measurements are not directly comparable to off-line measurement.

Attention (Ameritest)

This is a direct measure of a commercial's ability to win in the street fight for audience attention. The test ad is shown with control ads in a clutter reel environment designed to simulate a commercial "pod" on television. The test ad is embedded in clutter made up of either directly competitive advertising, or ads from non-competing product categories, depending on client preference. After watching the reel, respondents are asked the question, "Which of these ads did you find *interesting*?" If the test ad is spontaneously mentioned as one of the ads the respondent found interesting, that is counted toward the attention score. The same approach is used online as well as offline. While this measure is not a memory test of advertising, when combined with the measure of brand linkage it has been found to correlate well with awareness measures from recognition-based in-market tracking studies.

Attention (MSW)

This is a measure of the audience's ability to remember the test ad on an unaided basis after viewing it in a simulated program environment which also contains other control and test ads. While this breakthrough measure is based on a form of memory retrieval, published research suggests that the MSW is not correlated with day after recall scores and therefore is measuring something different. From the published literature, it is not yet known how it correlates with the other measures of attention described here.

Attention (Millward Brown)

This is a derived measure of an ad's ability to gain attention based in equal parts on two variables: 1) how enjoyable the ad is to watch (a rating scale) and 2) how actively the viewer is engaged by the execution (measured from three multiple choice questions). In the offline version, these questions are asked after a "warm-up" clutter reel; in the online version the clutter reel has been dropped. This measure was modeled from MB's extensive database of in-market continuous advertising tracking and generally produces a good fit—hence the name "link"—with MB measures of advertising awareness.

Attention (Ipsos-ASI)

This measure is collected after an audience has been exposed to test and control commercials embedded in a simulated program environment played in their home on a videotape. Twenty four hours later, respondents are read de-branded verbal descriptions of the commercials over the telephone and those who remember having seen the commercial are counted toward the Attention score. As a rule of thumb, the Attention score obtained from this form of verbal recognition will be roughly twice the level of the Recall score obtained from the same interview. Because verbal prompts are used for this "recognition" score, this measure generally correlates well with telephone based measures of advertising awareness from in market tracking studies.

Recall (Ipsos-ASI)

In this form of recall testing respondents are sent a videotape containing a simulated program and various control and test commercials and asked to watch it in their home. Respondents are then contacted 24 hours later and asked to recall all the advertising they remember seeing from a series of category and brand prompts. This measure also appears to correlate well with telephone based measures of ad awareness, though the correlation with actual in market sales has been debated vigorously over the years.

Recall (ARS)

In this form of recall testing respondents are invited to a theater, ostensibly to watch a pilot television program, which contains various control and test commercials. Respondents are then contacted 72 hours later and are asked to recall all the advertising they remember seeing from a series of category and brand prompts. (Note: the 72 hour period was selected for this test to calibrate the different levels of recall obtained from theater testing versus the original Burke on-air test which used a 24 hour "day after" forgetting time.) This measure also appears to correlate well with telephone based measures of ad awareness.

BRANDING

What is the role of the brand in the miniature movie that is a television commercial? Is it the star of the movie, driving the plot forward and occupying the center spotlight of consumer thoughts whether on screen or off? Is it a supporting actor, carrying a scene or two in the service of the action, providing essential information to make the story more interesting and relevant for the audience? Is it merely an extra playing a bit part in the movie? Or is it more like a director, only appearing in the credits at the end of the film?

If the role of advertising is to make ordinary products and services famous, then these casting questions are of paramount importance. From a research standpoint, this relates to the assessment of *how well a television commercial is branded.* Ultimately, we believe that consideration of this issue can also help inspire creative guidelines for producing well-branded commercials.

Many pre-testing systems report metrics with such labels as "branding" or "brand linkage." Not surprisingly, each system defines their "branding" construct using their own proprietary procedures, measures, or operations. And sometimes the measures that are created don't map tightly enough onto the theoretical constructs. For example, the Ipsos-ASI approach described below may be limited by their use of a verbal rather than a visual cue to commercial recognition, a primary component of their branding measure.

We must be careful to recognize that although the same "surface" label is being used, the "deep" constructs being measured are not necessarily equivalent.

In fact, published research suggests that the three approaches used to measure branding are uncorrelated, and therefore different from each other. Each might, in fact, be measuring some important facet of the complex problem of constructing well-branded advertising. The models that have been built to understand each of these branding measures suggest different approaches to achieving a good branding score. The Ipsos ASI approach, for example, suggests an "early and often rule"—showing the brand in the first few seconds of the ad to frame the communication and using brand name repetition to achieve a good branding score. In contrast, the Ameritest approach suggests that only a "single minded branding moment" is required: a peak visual moment somewhere in the commercial—it could be either at the beginning, the middle or even the end—where the attention of the audience is focused clearly on the identity of the brand. The Millward Brown approach suggests the importance of the audio component in achieving well branded advertising. Philosophically, all three approaches to measuring branding appear to have merit.

Ameritest Brand Linkage

This measure of branding is also similar to the unaided, or top-of-mind brand awareness measure generated by a traditional advertising tracking study. At the beginning of the interview, respondents are shown a clutter reel of five commercials, including the test commercial. (In the case of print, respondents are shown a clutter portfolio of ten print ads including the test ad.) Then the respondent is asked the question "Which of these ads did you find interesting?" If they mention the test ad as one of the interesting ads, the open-ended response to this question is coded for whether or not the respondent used the brand name. Brand Linkage, then, is the ratio of respondents spontaneously referencing the brand to the total number of respondents who found the ad interesting.

Since the respondent only has to retrieve the brand name from short-term memory, this measure is not really a memory test but rather is a measure of brand salience or how top-of-mind the brand is in being associated with the memory of the ad. Consequently, an appropriate metaphor for understanding this branding construct is that of a *handle* which the consumer uses to hold on to the experience created by well-branded advertising.

Ipsos-ASI Brand Linkage

Of the three pre-testing firms represented here, the Ipsos-ASI measure of brand linkage is the only derived measure, calculated from two other primary measures rather than measured directly. It is of particular theoretical interest because the two primary measures are Recall and Recognition. The Ipsos-ASI measure of Brand Linkage is the ratio of Recall to Recognition.

On a conceptual level, the Ipsos-ASI measure attempts to quantify the strength of the connection between two different memory systems where advertising content might be stored. Recall uses category and brand cues to retrieve memories from the semantic memory system. Recognition, by contrast, uses verbal descriptions of the ad to elicit the memory of the advertising from the episodic memory system which is then reported as an Attention score. In metaphorical terms, we might think of this measurement construct as the *bridge* between two memory systems.

Millward Brown Branding

This measure of branding is of major interest since it was specifically designed to line up with continuous advertising tracking data. Specifically, Millward Brown uses the mean of a five-point verbal scale ranging from "You couldn't help but remember this commercial is for (brand)" all the way to "It could be a commercial for almost anything."

The idea here is that advertising should avoid being generic. A poor ad is one in which you could substitute any brand in the category and it would remain the same. In contrast, a key diagnostic for this measure is that a well-branded ad is one in which, in open-ended playback, it is impossible for consumers to talk about the ad without talking about the brand. This measure of branding, therefore, is characterized by strong product/narrative integration. In metaphorical terms, we might think of this measurement construct as *tailor-made*. Advertising is like a suit that a brand wears; the well-dressed brand should wear a custom-tailored, "bespoke" suit rather than one ready-made right off the rack.

MOTIVATION AND PERSUASION

The difference between advertising film and entertainment film is that advertising has to *sell* something. For that reason, almost all pre-testing systems provide some measure of motivation or persuasiveness.

The role of motivation is not to be confused with the role of reason versus emotion in advertising, though it sometimes is. Motivation is not just a function of rational argument or persuasive selling propositions. Football coaches do not usually motivate their players with rational arguments.

Thought and emotion have a role to play in all pieces of advertising. One of the sources of confusion is that the balance between the two changes as the brand evolves over its lifestage.

For that reason, the benchmarks or norms used to interpret motivation scores usually take into account the lifestage of the brand. Most systems, for example, will provide a different normative comparison for new product advertising than for established brand advertising, since new product ads are seen as operating in a different way than established brand advertising. New product ads, for example, perform much more of a teaching role, showing the consumer what the brand looks like, how it fits into their world and how it differs from other alternatives in the category. Established brands, in contrast, are more focused on strengthening the loyalty of the relationship with the consumer, typically through emotional appeals rather than rational argument.

As an extension of the lifestage argument, a few companies also posit a third category for normative comparisons, the "power brand." These are brands that are so dominant in their market share—brands like Quaker Oats or

Microsoft Windows—that they play the role of leader in their category, trying to hold their category empire together rather than differentiating themselves on the basis of the secondary performance dimensions advertised by niche players.

Motivation (Ameritest)

Ameritest employs standard five point rating of consumer *intentions* toward the brand after viewing the ad, ranging from "definitely will" to "definitely will not." The wording of the question varies slightly depending on the advertised category: for consumer package goods, the question is purchase intent; for the automotive category, it is purchase consideration; for retail, it is intended store visits; for a media entertainment brand it is intention to view, etc. The motivation score gives the strongest weight to the top box or "definitely will buy" score. This measure is quite similar to that used by various concept tests or simulated test market systems, like the widely used BASES concept testing system. Because of the placement or location of the motivation question in the Ameritest interview immediately after forced exposure to the test ad, this measure is designed to respond to both the rational and emotional components of advertising. Norms are provided based on the lifestage of the brand—e.g., new products, established brands, "power" brands—as well as the category.

Motivation (Ipsos-ASI)

Similar to Ameritest, the ASI Motivation measure is usually a rating of consumer intentions to consider/visit/buy, depending on the category. Frequently, the ratings collected in the ad test is benchmarked against a "control" ad where the sample ratings are collected from a demographically matched sample of consumers who were not exposed to any advertising. By comparing the two ratings, it is possible to see how much the advertising has shifted the probability that consumers will purchase the brand.

Persuasion (Millward Brown)

This is one of two primary measures which gauge the consumer response to the advertising message. Persuasion is divided into a three part question, with slight differences in wording, depending on whether the respondent is a regular user of the brand, someone who has tried the brand but does not use it regularly, or a non-trier of the brand. Because of the placement or location of the persuasion question in the MB interview, this measure is designed to capture the "rational" response to the advertising, with the emotional response being captured by the enjoyment rating, so that the two measures when added together capture the total "effect" of the advertising.

Persuasion (ARS)

This is a "pre-post" measure of how the advertising shifts consumer intentions to purchase the brand. Before viewing the program in the theater, respondents are given envelopes containing a "photoshelf" of the brands in the test category and asked to indicate which brand they would prefer to win in a prize drawing. After viewing the program and advertising, respondents are given the photoshelf again and asked their preferences once more. Persuasion is calculated by subtracting the pre-ad exposure brand preference from their post-exposure preference. The benchmark against which this measure is compared is known as the Fair Share™ score—a modeled norm which takes into account factors such as how fragmented or competitive the category is and the brand's market share.

Persuasion (MSW)

Similar to ARS, the MSW measure of persuasion is based on a pre-exposure to post-ad exposure shift in consumer intentions to select the advertised brand from a "photo shelf" of competing alternatives.

COMPOSITE MEASURES

Composite measures exist as a matter of convenience. These "single" number measures are designed to make it easy for senior managers of an organization to keep track of the many ads they are responsible for, possibly in many different countries, and to communicate to other non-research oriented senior managers the performance of that advertising.

Composite measures are not designed to provide insights or understanding of an ad's performance, but simply to provide a headline for the ad's performance in an elevator conversation.

The various composite measures that different systems provide, therefore, do not represent new measurement and are subject to the same criticisms and limitations of the component measures.

Ameritest Performance Index [API] (Ameritest):

This is calculated by combining Branded Attention (which is itself the product of Brand Linkage and Attention) with Weighted Motivation, then indexing it against the average of the relevant distribution of API scores (e.g., all :30 ads, all :15 ads, etc.). Ameritest reports both the Index of the API as well as it's decile in the distribution of APIs against which it's being compared. Conceptually, this means that an effective ad must break through the clutter, be well-branded and motivate the consumer to purchase the product or use the service.

Awareness Index (Millward Brown)

A measure designed to predict the incremental impact of a TV commercial on advertising awareness—as measured in the marketplace by one of Millward Brown's continuous trackers.

For example, an Awareness index of 1 would generate 1 additional point of ad awareness per 100 GRP's, if the base level is zero. (When base level is non-zero, the predicted gain is less than 1 point per 100 GRP's.) The AI score is derived from a combination of pre-test measures of enjoyment, involvement (memorability) and Branding. The AI is a component of Millward Brown's Effectiveness Index (EI) which also takes the ad's persuasiveness into account.

Copy Effect Index (Ipsos-ASI):

This is calculated by combining measures of Recall and Persuasion that have been previously indexed to their respective norms. Conceptually, this means that effective advertising must be both memorable and persuasive.

Effectiveness Index [EI] (Millward Brown):

This is calculated by summing a weighted combination of Attention, Branding and Communication Effect (a measure that in itself includes Persuasion and Enjoyment).

Conceptually, this means that an effective ad must break through the clutter, be well-branded and must motivate the consumer either rationally or on an emotional level.

Liking

Liking is strongly correlated with both Attention and Motivation, and therefore is related to the sales effectiveness of advertising. The relationship between Liking and Recall is more problematic, with some studies showing a negative relationship between Liking and Recall and others show little or no correlation.

Commercials that are liked tend to be entertaining and also tend to convey relevant, believable, brand differentiating messages. But knowing that you have a well-liked execution does not tell you, by itself, what it is about the commercial that is liked: the commercial execution or the advertising message?

Recognition vs Recall: Tracking Advertising in the Marketplace

You are at a party. You see someone smiling and coming toward you, and you know that you've met that person before—you clearly recognize the face—but you just can't recall the person's name! It's a simple memory test that reminds us that the human mind stores memories in more than one way. For advertising researchers, it triggers the debate about the relative merits of *recognition vs. recall* as Attention measures of advertising awareness.

The logic of much of the research that is conducted on advertising is that for it to be effective, it must leave some kind of trace in the memory of the consumer. But what kind of trace? Think about our hypothetical party for a moment. Which is proof that you have or have not met the person before: the fact that you *Recognize* the face or the fact that you can't *Recall* their name?

It doesn't seem surprising that in the case of in-market tracking, the measure of awareness of a specific advertising campaign using *recognition* can be substantially different from a measure based on *recall*. It is sometimes higher by as much as a factor of two! Which measure should you believe?

Most people would trust their recognition memory system more than they would trust their ability to recall things such as names. While some people might have minds as orderly and indexed as a library card catalog, most minds are better described by a concept that the French call a "gallimaufry"—a hodgepodge or jumble. It's like the junk drawer in the kitchen of the mind. Retrieving a memory from such mental gallimaufry requires a time consuming search.

This helps explain why, in response to recall questions, consumers will sometimes play back images from ads that haven't aired in twenty years and yet completely fail to mention a campaign that our client just spent twenty million dollars airing. Or they will sometimes describe a competitor's ad as one of our client's because they filed it away in memory under the wrong index heading.

One of the main advantages of using the Internet for studying advertising is that it allows you to put something in front of the eyes of consumers to test whether or not they recognize the "face" of the advertising. While some telephone tracking studies have attempted to produce a "recognition" measure by reading a verbal description of advertising over the phone, it's quite obvious that this substitute approach is no more reliable than it would be for you to help me find a particular face in a crowd if all you had to go on was a one or two sentence description of what that face looks like. Using a verbal cue to get at visual recognition is simply not very effective.

And yet, in the United States, *recall* measures of advertising awareness have been the dominant approach used for at least the past quarter century. Why? Because historically, telephone surveys conducted by large cost-efficient telephone centers were the most economical way of interviewing a projectable sample of consumers. The Internet now provides a viable alternative.

IV

Leading Audience Attention

IV

Leading Audience Attention

Two books share a core metaphor and provide important lessons for advertising practitioners: *Blink*, by Malcolm Gladwell, and *In the Blink of an Eye*, by Walter Murch. These books provide valuable insights into how an audience experiences advertising film—and ultimately, in how brand images get built.

Gladwell is a best-selling science journalist who writes about the new science of rapid cognition, the role of the unconscious mind in decision making. Murch is an award winning Hollywood film editor who has worked on such movies as *American Graffiti, The Godfather Part II, Apocalypse Now, Ghost* and *The English Patient*. As one of the leading craftsmen of the cinematic art form, Murch describes his work habits and esthetic theories.

Gladwell is creating quite a stir in advertising circles because of his science based defense of the role of the "gut" in effective decision making. Along with more academic thinkers, such as Gerald Zaltman of Harvard, he writes about the theory of the "adaptive unconscious." This is the notion that up to 95% of the decisions we make everyday are outside of our conscious field of attention. The mind is thought of as a kind of giant computer that quickly and quietly processes a lot of the data behind the scenes while we focus on a few icons on our cerebral desktop.

A blink is a particularly apt metaphor for this theory because of its reference to the eye. A large body of research supports the idea of the intelligent eye. It has been shown that a very large part of the brain is devoted to constructing—not simply recording—what we think of as visual perception.

As we watch television, the eye actively filters film images—on a pre-conscious level—deciding what to let into the conscious mind, and into long term memory, to form those images associated with a brand. It's a snap-decision process, like the way you sort through the junk mail arriving in your mailbox, when you decide in a fraction of a second to toss a piece of advertising unopened into the trash can or set aside the letter from the IRS to look at later. As a defense mechanism, the eye has evolved efficient anti-spam filters to avoid sensory overload.

If you stop to think about it, without such pre-conscious filtering you wouldn't be able to drive a car. At even a moderate speed, as you look through the windshield at the road, thousands of pieces of information from the outside world are competing for your attention: the oncoming traffic, the bicyclist, the pedestrian about to cross the street, the signal light up ahead about to change color, the car getting ready to make the left turn, the voice over from the passenger in the seat next to yours, the number on the house you're searching for, and so on. Without the ability to filter and focus on the street scene ahead of you, you'd quickly have an accident.

According to Gladwell, the reason we can do this is because of how our minds "thin-slice" the information that we take in. Gladwell says,

> *"'Thin-slicing' refers to the ability of our unconscious to find patterns in situations and behavior based on very narrow slices of experience."*

In terms of film, we as an audience are using the same pre-conscious ability of thin slicing as we participate in the process of making meaning. Gladwell tells a story in Blink of how the scientist Paul Ekman, an expert in reading faces, deconstructed a film of Kato Kaelin's testimony in the O.J. Simpson trial and demonstrated thin slicing in action. By taking apart the film down to a single frame, one moment stood out from the others. During hostile questioning by the attorney Marcia Clark, Kato's face was utterly transformed. His otherwise passive face was caught in that "slice" of film with teeth bared, eyebrows lowered. Ekman described him as "a snarling dog."

As all editors and filmmakers know, this deconstruction is vital to the process of story-telling through film. From a filmmaking perspective, the art of editing lies in determining how to cut the visual information in film into meaningful slices of experience.

Walter Murch considers the discovery that our visual experience could be thin-sliced as the defining moment in the history of film. He states,

> *"The discovery early in the century that certain kinds of cutting 'worked' led almost immediately to the discovery that films could be shot discontinuously, which was the cinematic equivalent of the discovery of flight."*

Anyone who has watched an unedited home movie can see why editing is so important to the success of movies. Yet it was not obvious to early film-makers that slicing up visual experience and rejoining them in a way that violates the continuity of "real life" would be anything but confusing. After all, if the "wholeness" of experience was divided, wouldn't something of the essence be lost? Murch continues,

> *"The mysterious part of it, though, is that the joining of those pieces—the 'cut' in American terminology—actually does seem to work, even though it represents a total and instantaneous displacement of one field of vision with another, a displacement that sometimes also entails a jump forward or backward in time as well as space."*

While their business is making movies and not writing books about the psychology behind the movies, experienced film artists must operate with at least implicit psychological theories about why they do what they do. One of the greatest film directors of all time, John Huston, gave this down-to-earth description of the psychological nature of the cut in an interview, which Murch quotes in his book:

> *"Look at that lamp across the room. Now look back at me. Look back at that lamp. Now look back at me again. Do you see what you did? You blinked. Those are the cuts. After the first look, you know that there's no reason to pan continuously from me to the lamp because you know what's in between. Your mind cut the scene. First you behold the lamp. Cut. Then you behold me."*

Indeed, much of the art of editing film lies in controlling the discontinuities of thin slices of film experience. As Murch explains,

> *"We must render visual reality discontinuous; otherwise perceived reality would resemble an almost incomprehensible string of letters without word separation or punctuation."*

The cut in film is comparable to the essential role of the gutter in a comic strip. It is into that infinitely thin space between two adjacent but distinct slices of experience that the audience's imagination enters in order to close the gap in continuity. It is here that audience's imagination participates, on equal terms with the filmmaker, in co-creating the meaning of the film.

Together, the filmmaker and the audience are engaged in a creative dance. The job of the filmmaker is to "lead" his dance partner from one idea or emotion to the next. As Murch points out,

> *"Your job is partly to anticipate, partly to control the thought processes of the audience. To give them what they want and/or what they need just before they have to 'ask' for it—to be surprising yet self-evident at the same time."*

All together, Murch describes six criteria for what makes a good cut as follows,

> *"An ideal cut (for me) is the one that satisfies all of the following six criteria at once: 1) it is true to the emotion of the moment; 2) it advances the story; 3) it occurs at a moment that is rhythmically interesting and 'right'; 4) it acknowledges what you might call 'eye-trace'—the concern with the location and movement of the audience's focus of interest within the frame; 5) it respects 'planarity'—the grammar of three dimensions transposed by photography to two (the question of stage-line, etc); 6) and it respects the three-dimensional continuity of the actual space."*

Emotion is the most important of these to Murch by far. And for that reason it is interesting to describe the work habits he has developed over time for keeping track of the emotions he is trying to create in the film.

As part of his preparation for a project he creates a visual vocabulary for the emotional language of the film he is working on. He does this by taking still photographs from the raw film that has been shot. Murch states,

> *"But in addition to the usual procedures, I also would select at least one representative frame from every setup and take a still photograph of it off the workprint. ...and they were put onto panels arranged according to scene..."*

The reason he does this is that he understands intuitively the limitations of language. Words, while they are important, cannot capture all of the esthetic information contained in a picture. Murch continues,

> *"...the most interesting asset of the photos for me was that they provided the hieroglyphs for a language of emotions. What word expresses the concept of ironic anger tinged with melancholy? There isn't a word for it, in English anyway, but you can see that specific emotion represented in this photograph."*

Gladwell's purpose in using still photographs is "to embody the nameless but familiar emotion I see in that photograph." The still photographs provide a set of keys to the emotions flowing through the film experience he is constructing. Murch explains,

> *"In choosing a representative frame, what you're*
> *looking for is an image that distills the essence of*
> *the thousands of frames that make up the shot in*
> *question, what Cartier-Bresson—referring to still*
> *photography—called the 'decisive moment.' So I*
> *think, more often than not, the image that I chose*
> *wound up in the film. And also, more often than*
> *not, quite close to the cut point."*

The heart of the art of editing lies in developing an intuitive feel for the "right" time to make the cut. That requires a feel for the response of the filmmaker's creative partner, the audience.

Early film theorists suggested that a cut should be made at the peak of the "content curve," which is the point in the shot at which the audience has been able to absorb most of its information. Cut too soon and the audience gets confused; wait too long and the film begins to drag and gets boring. According to Murch, the blink is tied to the audience's comprehension,

> *"I believe you will find that your listener will blink*
> *at the precise moment he or she 'gets' the idea of*
> *what you are saying, not an instant earlier or later."*

Blinks occur at focal points of audience attention. They correspond to the idea of the "beat" in music; in acting, the beat is also used to describe the emotional transactions between two actors performing the dialogue in a scene.

An actor who is fully engaged in a scene can react to unpredictable events "without missing a beat." Similarly, in film the visual "beat" is the emotional or informational transaction between the filmmaker and the audience. A sequence of such peak moments of audience attention gives rise to structure in the flow of experience.

The importance of rhythmic structure in communication extends beyond film.Cognitive researchers, for example, have commented on the importance of rhythm and beat in language to help us organize the information in a conversation to avoid cognitive overload by focusing on predictable, strategic moments to pay attention. In spoken language, for instance, the words you stress are the important ones, and you automatically speed up or slow down on the words in between so that the major points of stress form a regular chain of beats. The beat is when speakers often convey key information and bring up new topics.

In advertising film, the visual beat of the film is strongly related to the attention-getting power and the recall score of a television commercial. Research published by Ameritest shows that the number of peak moments, or visual beats, is the single best predictor of a TV commercial's ability to break through clutter. The number of visual beats is tied to narrative structure, how the film is edited to involve the audience. For example, good stories are generally characterized by more beats.

The same research shows that the difference between attention and recall is the type of information content of the visual beats of the ad film.

Ads that do well on day-after recall tests will focus the audience attention on product-related information, such as visualizations of the consumer need, product attributes, product demos, the package or the brand name. This is not surprising, since recall testing is based on the theory that advertising works by "teaching" you something about the product. In fact, that's where recall tests came from originally—your teacher taught you a lesson on Wednesday and gave you a recall test on Friday to see if you learned anything.

In contrast to recall, attention scores are driven by the esthetic or emotional content of the ad. The images in the visual beat of the film may not show the product, but by engaging the attention and emotions of the audience they can still make a profitable contribution to the brand's image. Indeed, recent research on a successful ad campaign has shown that the images that occur in those visual beats—and not any of the other images from the commercial—can still be found in the memories of consumers up to five years after the commercial has gone off air. So, it appears that those peak moments are where the long term work of advertising is being done: creating brands.

Using the same techniques we use for advertising film, we thin-sliced the film experience of a classic silent film, *The Tramp*, (See the exhibit at the end of this chapter). Looking at the Flow of Attention, you can see the editing rhythm of the film through the eyes of the audience. In this thirty seven minute movie there are twelve major peaks of audience interest that stand out above all the other images in the film. And what, do you suppose, is the irresistible magnet for the eye of the audience? The brand: Charlie Chaplin.

Many in the advertising community who have embraced Gladwell's book on the grounds that you should "trust your instincts" have overlooked one of the important lessons of the book. Gladwell says,

> *"Our unconscious is a powerful force. But it's fallible. It's not the case that our internal computer always shines through, instantly decoding the 'truth' of a situation. It can be thrown off, distracted, and disabled."*

For researchers the story about how it was possible for ordinary people to obtain insights into the operations of the subconscious is particularly salient. *Blink* tells the story of a researcher who developed a complex model to predict whether or not couples would get divorced over time by analyzing videotapes of them having conversations. As a training exercise, the researcher took a number of couples' videos and showed them to non-experts. The researcher thin-sliced the videos into very short sections, and gave them a simple list of emotions to look for. What happened? The non-experts predicted with 80% accuracy which marriages were going to make it.

The potential contribution of research to the creative process appears to be a belief shared by Walter Murch as follows,

> "Toward the end of the editing process on Julia, Fred Zimmerman observed that he felt the director and the editor, alone with the film for months and months, could only go ninety percent of the way toward the finished film—that what was needed for the last ten percent was 'the participation of the audience', who he saw as his final collaborators. Not in the sense that he would respond to them blindly, but that he felt their presence was helpful as a corrective, to keep certain obsessions from becoming corrosive and to point out blind spots that may have developed through over-familiarity with the material."

Toward this end, Murch urges a certain kind of "virginity"—the ability to see the movie as if for the first time. He states,

> "The editor, on the other hand, should try to see only what's on the screen, as the audience will."

Gladwell and Murch have contributed valuable insights into exactly how rapid cognition and film work. Expertise in making advertising films, and in-depth knowledge about a brand—these give individuals the expertise Gladwell talks about, the kind that can often enable reliable and extraordinarily fast decisions. Yet, it is the product of that expertise that must thrive away from home and out in the world. In the final analysis, it is the audience whose advertising experience matters and who will, or will not, create a vigorous brand.

If researchers have one thing to add above all else, it's audience experience. The analysis of thousands of commercials have demonstrated without ambiguity that audiences, taught from childhood how to watch films, have an expertise of their own to add, and they do it in the blink of an eye.

The Ameritest Flow of Attention graph makes visible the rhythms of visual storytelling. This is an audience analysis of the 37-minute film classic, "The Tramp." On this graph, the height of each picture tells you the percentage of the audience that is paying attention to a particular image. Notice how the star, Charlie Chaplin, is the focus of audience attention—his image occurs in most of the memorable storytelling peaks. Peak moments are key to understanding how the structure and drama of film creates an emotional experience. In TV advertising, the same creative process is used to make products famous and build brand image.

V

Four Dramatic Structures of Emotional TV Advertising

V

Four Dramatic Structures of Emotional TV Advertising

On an intellectual level, television commercials work by telling us what we are supposed to think about a product or service; but on another level they work by showing us how we are supposed to feel about a brand. Good storytelling, which unites ideas with emotions, lies at the heart of advertising effectiveness. For television, that means constructing a visually compelling story with moving pictures.

In a recent interview with the *Harvard Business Review* (Fryer, 2003), Robert McKee, one of the most respected screenwriting lecturers in Hollywood, discussed some of the structural principles involved in telling a good story and pointed out the benefits of applying this knowledge to the practice of management. Most executives make the mistake of attempting to persuade using lectures replete with statistics, facts, litanies of bullet points and quotes from authorities. McKee argues convincingly that executives could be more persuasive using dramas—compelling stories packed with emotional power. For the ad business, understanding the role of the brand in the context of the different structures of storytelling lies at the heart of how to analyze a television commercial.

Along similar lines to McKee, the ad researcher Bill Wells classified all television commercials into two fundamental types: lectures and dramas. This simple categorization brought some clarity to the debate about the role of reason and emotion in advertising. While the lecture type tends to be simply a linear presentation of features and benefits designed to convey a rational argument for buying the brand—a unique selling proposition—when we talk about dramas (both light and comic, as well as those more serious in emotional tonality) we must recognize that structural issues are more complex. Good stories can be told in more than one way.

In fact, from the Ameritest pre-testing experience we have identified four distinct structures associated with effective emotional advertising. The role of the brand in each of these four types of stories is quite different.

THE FLOW OF EMOTION
AND PERFORMANCE MEASURES ON PRETESTS

To explain these four structures we must first describe how we go about measuring the emotion in television commercials. For McKee, "a story expresses how and why life changes." To measure the emotion generated by a commercial story, therefore, requires a dynamic variable, one that captures how the audience's feelings change as they move through the film. We call the measure we use the Flow of Emotion.

The metaphor employed here is to model emotion as a "fluid" which is pumped through an ad—that is, the more emotionally engaging a commercial is visually, the more volume of emotion is pumped in. To slightly expand the metaphor, emotion is thought of as coming in two flavors, positive and negative, so that the dynamic tension between the two can be analyzed to understand the dramatic structure of a particular commercial. We visualize that structure by creating a graphic representation by

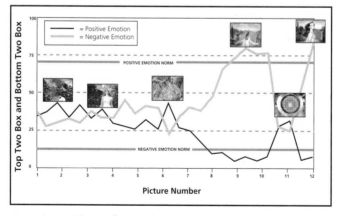

Ameritest Flow of Emotion graph.

superimposing two curves: one represents the percent of respondents who choose the top two boxes (positive end of the scale) and the other represents the percent choosing the bottom two boxes (negative end of the scale).

The average level of these positive and negative flows is the area under each of the two curves. The relationship between these averages and commercial performance measures on two pre-testing systems used by Unilever is shown in the table below.

	Positive Flow of Emotion	Negative Flow of Emotion
Liking	0.46[1]	-0.51[2]
Ameritest Measures		
Attention	-0.08	0.13
Branding	0.19[1]	-0.24[2]
Communication (strategic message playback)	0.31[2]	-0.21[2]
Motivation (weighted purchase intent)	0.58[2]	-0.57[2]
Millward Brown Measures		
Attention	-0.17[1]	0.33[2]
Branding	0.29[2]	-0.27[2]
Communication Effect	0.51[2]	-0.59[2]
Overall Effectiveness Index	0.44[2]	-0.33[2]

Notes: [1]Significance >95% confidence, [2]Significance >99% confidence.
N = 68 Unilever commercial's

The Flow of Emotion does not strongly predict attention-getting power but it is strongly predictive of motivation or persuasion. This is highly desirable since attention and motivation are conceptually distinct constructs. It is easy to think of commercials that break through the clutter but don't motivate you to buy, as well as those that have a compelling strategic message but don't get your attention. However, there is a significant relationship between the emotion flows and both measures of branding and an even stronger statistical relationship between the emotion flows and measures of communication effectiveness and motivation (for example, purchase intent).

We interpret this to be like the concept of "working energy" in physics, where the distinction is made between the total energy of a system and the energy available to do work. The total emotional energy of an ad may contain a component of entertainment value or even borrowed interest for the purposes of attracting attention, but the flow of emotion as measured here relates primarily to the 'working emotion' in the system that is available to build the brand and to sell products.

Four Dramatic Structures

The dramatic structure of a television commercial may be thought of as organized emotion. In our pretesting work we have identified four types of emotional organization or dramatic structures which, in general, can be found in effective commercials (commercials that have scored well on pre-test performance measures)—the Emotional Pivot, the Positive Transition, the

Build, and Sustained Emotion, as shown below.

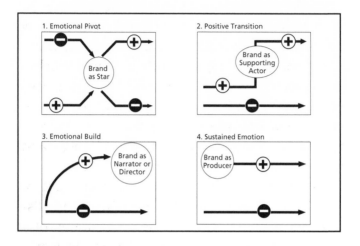

The Emotional Pivot

This dramatic structure involves a "phase transition" in audience emotional states, from a beginning negative state to an ending positive state. It is characterized by strong negative emotion ratings in the beginning of the execution, which then vanish abruptly and are replaced by strong positive emotions by the end of the ad. The point in the ad where the negative emotions flip over to positive emotions is called the "emotional pivot." Problem/ solution commercials are one genre of advertising which have this type of emotional structure.

The Positive Transition

This structure also involves an abrupt or

discontinuous change in emotional states, but this time from a low-level positive state to a higher level positive state—like an energy jump in quantum mechanics. Thus, the flow graph for this type of execution looks like a step function. Executions that make use of a reveal technique, where there is a moment of sudden realization that the ad is about something completely different that what one originally thought, provide examples of this type of dramatic structure.

The Build

The third type of dramatic structure involves a smoothly increasing flow of positive audience feelings climaxing in an emotional high point at the end of the ad. Humorous commercials with a strong visual payoff produce examples of this type.

Sustained Emotion

The fourth structure represents commercials that simply make you feel good from beginning to end. The flow graph shows a high positive, but flat pattern, indicative of a high volume of emotion being pumped through the ad. Montage commercials with strong music tracks yield examples of this type.

It should be noted that lecture type ads will look like this last type of emotional ad in terms of the flow graph, with the main difference being that the focus of audience attention in the ad is on rational information content rather than esthetic or emotional content.

Each of these structures may be thought of as an elementary building block which in longer pieces of film may be combined in different ways to create more complex stories, though most thirty second commercials are short enough that they represent fairly pure examples of each of these types.

In analyzing an ad, we should also be careful to distinguish between emotional effects intended by the creative—the purposeful use of negative emotions in an emotional pivot—versus unintended effects that represent opportunities for polishing or improving the ad. Our extensive pretesting experience has often shown that sub-optimal commercials—i.e., those that fail to meet or exceed hurdles or norms for Attention, Branding, Communication, and Motivation—don't introduce the brand at the proper time so it can "take credit" for an emotional pivot, or alternatively, use an unclear, disorganized or incompletely realized dramatic structure.

Four Different Roles of the Brand

Notice that in two of the four dramatic structures the brand identifier is introduced in the middle of the commercial, as part of the action in the film, while in the other two structures the brand is a book-end, either at the beginning or the end of the ad. The timing of the introduction of brand identifiers—e.g., package, name, logo—is key to defining the role of the brand in the four different structures. A simple way of thinking about the differences is to think of the brand in terms of four different Hollywood types.

Brand as Star

The most obvious role for the brand is that of the star of the little movie that is a television commercial. In this type of drama, the emotional pivot, the plot is quite simple. Negative dramatic tension is created in the beginning of the ad, then the brand arrives on its white horse and makes the negative feelings go away, so that the audience leaves with a happy ending. If the brand arrives at just the right time in the story, which is at the boundary between the negative emotional state and the positive emotional state, then the brand receives the credit and is perceived as the cause of this change or resolution of emotional tension. The brand clearly becomes the hero of the spot.

Brand as Supporting Actor

In this second type of story, the positive transition, the brand is not the star but plays the role of supporting actor. It is the Sancho Panza to the consumer's Don Quixote. The consumer, by projection, is given the starring role. The brand is part of the action, however, necessary to advance the scene and create twists in the plot. The role of the sporty car in some automotive advertising, for example, is to take ordinary life and elevate it to a higher plane of experience— which is, in the end, the promise the brand is making to the consumer as driver. Again, timing is a key point with this type of dramatic structure: the brand should arrive at the boundary between the low emotion state and the higher emotion state—so that the brand receives the credit and is perceived as the cause of the enhanced consumer experience.

Brand as Director

In this third type of story, the build, the brand is not an actor in the story but is acknowledged in only the credits at the end of the film. The brand is the director, unseen but an always-present intelligence, building a story to give meaning or definition to the experience promised to the consumer. Many of the IBM blue letterbox commercials are of the director type.

Brand as Producer

The fourth type—the thrilling exciting hilarious celebration of amazing sights and sounds you've never seen before—brought to you by—presented to you by—the brand!

It's the brand as the producer of sustained emotions, the rock concert promoter of good vibes, the P.T. Barnum of emotional end benefits. And it's up front about telling you so. No shyness here. (But remember, substitute rational selling propositions for emotions in this model and—hey presto!—you suddenly have brand as lecturer.)

SUMMARY

All four approaches to emotional advertising work effectively in the sense of scoring well on measures of performance, yet these four types represent a considerable repertoire for deploying emotions in the service of building brands. This analysis is confirmation of the idea that advertising can work in more than one way, particularly on an emotional level. What this means from a practical perspective is that creatives should be empowered to depict and to attempt to evoke the full spectrum of human emotion, from despondence to elation. It is also a reminder to students of advertising—and good storytelling—that structure and content are also important, regardless of the type of advertising we are talking about.

VI

Film Tips for Branding Television Commercials

VI

Film Tips for Branding Television Commercials

We have all had the experience of hearing someone say, "I saw a great commercial on television last night but I'm not sure who it was for." The reaction of a professional to that statement is to conclude that the advertiser probably just wasted money because the essence of great advertising is that it builds brands. Advertising that does not communicate the identity of the brand in a memorable way cannot be great advertising, no matter how entertaining or emotionally arousing the film is. Brand Linkage is the business concept that the experience of a television commercial should be linked somehow to the experience of a brand in order to grow the business.

WHY IS BRAND LINKAGE IMPORTANT?

It is quite possible that unbranded advertising could drive sales in a category. That's why it's become popular in recent years to use television advertising to sell milk or raisins or a drug-free lifestyle. But if a commercial sells without branding, its sales message and the benefits of that advertising will be expected to accrue to all the players in the category in proportion to the market share they currently have. To gain competitive advantage, a commercial must be branded. An effectively branded commercial will grow an advertiser's share of market in addition to any possible effects it has on the size of the market. Put simply, an effectively branded commercial will increase an advertiser's slice of the category pie, and if the pie grows too, so much the better!

FILM TIPS TO ENHANCE BRAND LINKAGE

The key to visual communication is understanding that all communication is interactive. Half of the experience of watching a television commercial is what ideas and images the advertiser puts into the ad. The other half is what the viewer brings to the party based on his or her own life experience, beliefs and attitudes. That's why up-front strategic research is so important to the communications process. Visual perception is not a passive recording of stimulus material. The eye is not a camera, rather it is an active processor of visual information. According to an old saw, "...there is no such thing as immaculate perception." Visually effective advertising that builds brands begins with a proper respect for the intelligent eye of the viewer.

The following guidelines are based on

research findings from the study of the flow of viewer attention to the visuals in literally hundreds of television commercials. These are not intended to be hard and fast rules for commercial filmmaking, but merely summarize our experience with what works in television advertising. Keep in mind that if you choose to ignore any particular guideline in a commercial that you are creating, you should do so deliberately, breaking rules in order to achieve the intended creative effect that you have in mind.

Visualization: Visualize the brand identity, don't just say it in the copy.

While it's obvious, it's so important that it bears repeating. Since television is primarily a visual medium, the key to effective Brand Linkage is visualization. If you have a problem with Brand Linkage in a commercial, trying to fix it by only making changes to the copy usually doesn't work. What follows are visual examples of "branding moments" in advertising.

In each of the following examples, the brand name is prominently displayed in a direct package shot or logo shot, and is the central focus of the visual.

Framing: Establish the category frame of
reference as soon as possible.

Just as framing a picture is important for
achieving a particular aesthetic effect, framing
the communication of ideas in a commercial is
important for achieving a branding effect. At
the beginning of a commercial you can be sure
the viewer's mind is anywhere but where you
want it to be. The average respondent is not
waiting to receive a message from you, or from
any other brand. To prepare each member of
the audience to receive a message from the
brand, it is important to provide category cues
early so that the viewer will be in the correct
frame of mind for processing the communication correctly.

The example shown below is the opening shot
for a hair care commercial. It provides explicit
visual cues that set up the viewer to expect
further information about the hair care product
category.

The major exception to this rule is the
Reveal, which is the technique of deliberately

keeping the viewer in the dark or off balance about the real subject of the commercial until very late in the commercial in order to achieve a dramatic, surprise ending. The reveal is particularly useful for old, established brands where the execution is used to draw non-users in to take a "second look at the brand" since cuing the brand too early may cause non-users, who think they've already made up their minds about the brand, to tune out.

Continuity: Create a unified selling proposition.
Continuity consists of weaving the threads of the different ideas in the commercial together in order to create a unified whole. The most obvious continuity structure from the world of filmmaking is the convention of beginning a sequence with a wide shot, cutting to a medium shot and finally to a close-up. To translate this idea into the world of advertising, you need to remember that continuity consists of weaving together different selling ideas into a unified selling proposition.

In the example above, continuity in constructing a selling proposition would consist of beginning a sequence with a categorical situation, cutting to the brand, and finally delivering the sales message. Another example of a continuity device would be a problem-solution commercial. Montage, another continuity device, involves the use of multiple brief images that express and often emphasize a single meaning or brand emotion. MTV type montage advertising can be quite effective, but only if continuity is maintained by focusing single-mindedly on one branding idea. Violations of continuity, or the "logic of the sale," are often root causes of problems with Brand Linkage.

Focusing: Make sure the brand is in a single-minded focal point of viewer attention at least once in the ad.

Just as in composing a photograph, some elements in the picture will be in the foreground creating the focal points of a viewer's attention, and other elements will be in the background creating context. The same is true of a television commercial. The only difference is that the focal points of attention exist in time, rather than in space. The primary use of the Flow of Attention graph is to identify what images are in the foreground of audience thoughts and attention (images that are relatively high on the curve), and what images remain in the background of the audience thoughts and attention (images that are relatively low on the curve).

The key to effective Brand Linkage is that, for at least one clear moment in the thirty-second flow of images, the brand is in the center of the field of viewer consciousness. This is the branding image to which all the other thoughts and feelings created in the film will be linked.

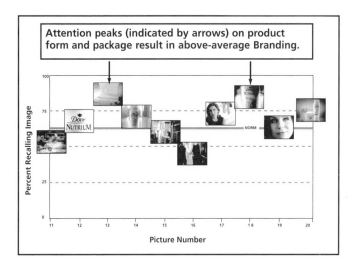

Transitions: Lead the viewer's attention to the brand. Shots exist in relation to other shots. When considering the placement of the brand in the flow of images in the commercial, it is necessary to consider the rhythm of ideas that come before and after.

The concept of rhythm is connected with that of expectation. Rhythm implies that after one event occurs in the Flow of Attention, the viewer expects the following event. It is essential to note that the looking forward is not with certainty, but with expectation.

Discontinuities in the Flow of Attention generally occur when the sequence of ideas and images changes direction unexpectedly, without a proper transition. For example, simply cutting to a shot of the brand at an unexpected moment in the flow can result in poor recall for that brand image and weakens Brand Linkage.

In an example of the Flow of Attention results for a Suave hair care commercial ("Loft" :30 shown below), the party scenes are not well integrated. Moreover, the "hair beauty" shots are tuned out by the viewer. All

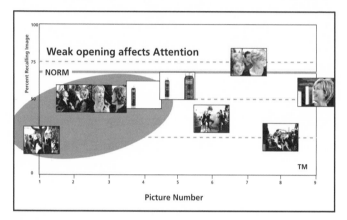

Flow of Attention for "Loft" :30, page 1 of 2.

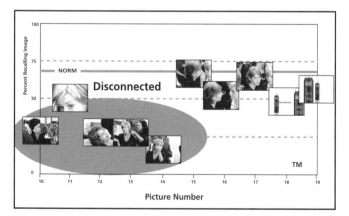

Flow of Attention for "Loft" :30, page 2 of 2.

of this disrupts attention and creates disconnects for the viewer.

Camera Distance: Use close-ups to move the viewer emotionally closer to the brand.

Camera distance is one of the key factors determining emotional response to the shot. Close-ups create an emotional intimacy or emphasis. More distant shots are cooler emotionally. Since one of the more important goals of advertising is to create an emotional bond between the customer and the brand, control of camera distance should be used to modulate the emotional distance between your customer and the brand. For example, as a visual rehearsal of the brand adoption process, you might use the camera to move viewer perceptions from the cooler, more rational and distant perceptions of the non-user of the brand to the close, emotional attachment of the brand's core user.

Zooming: Zoom in to make the viewer read the brand name, zoom out to shift attention to the visual.

Similar to the process of cutting from wide to medium to close-up, zooming in with a camera is a process of focusing the viewer's attention. Zooming in on a brand name (or a set of words in general) has the psychological effect of causing the viewer to read what's on screen. Conversely, zooming out shifts attention to the visual gestalt of what's on screen. Think of this camera technique in terms of the process of being drawn into a book versus stepping back in a museum to look at a picture hanging on the wall. In the example shown below, as we go from the first shot to the second shot, the camera is zooming in on the product to focus attention on reading the brand name.

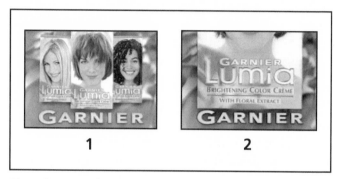

Zooming in *enhances reading and Branding scores improve.*

Camera Movement: Avoid panning across the letters of the brand name.

Panning across a long brand name is sometimes done to take advantage of the power of film to make the name feel more dynamic. However, this is a technique that may not create strong Brand Linkage. When people read, they perceive whole words as a gestalt and do not visually take in words one letter at a time.

Camera Angle: Avoid low angle shots of the brand.

Unusual camera angles can evoke strong viewer

emotions but they can also be confusing and imply unintended symbolic messages. Low angle shots of the brand convey power and authority, but also imply the attitude that the brand is talking down to the customer.

Within the frame: Avoid divided attention within the frame.

Because the amount of time that a given frame is on screen is under the control of the advertiser and not the viewer, you should not assume that the viewer will focus on more than one thought within the frame. In theory, copy and image should express a single thought.

An example of "in-frame" competition for attention. The yellow product in the lower-right corner fights the yellow tee-shirt to gain attention in this frame.

Duration: Pause on the brand to enhance attention.

The actual threshold of perception for registering a stimulus such as the brand varies as a function of several factors from the contrast in the image to the response time of the particular viewer. The longer the brand is on screen, the more likely it is to become a focal point in the flow of attention as the image "burns in" to viewer attention. In other words, pausing on the brand is a good way to enhance attention. As a general rule, a brand that is on screen for less than half a second is unlikely to register with the majority of your audience.

Tempo: Register the brand on the beat of the editing tempo.

Getting the editing tempo right is one of the most artful and intuitive parts of filmmaking. In a sense, the film editor is engaged in a kind of virtual dance with the viewer. You can lead, but the viewer must follow. The importance of rhythmic structure in all forms of communication has been studied by a number of researchers. Rhythm and beat in language, for example, help us to organize the information in a face-to-face conversation to avoid cognitive overload by focusing on predictable, strategic moments in which to pay attention. In spoken language, the words you stress are the important ones, and you automatically speed up or slow down on the words in between so that the major points of stress form a regular chain of beats. Researchers have found that the beat is when speakers often convey key information and bring up new topics.

An early film theorist, Raymond Spotiswoode, suggested that a cut should be made at the peak of the "content curve," which is the point in the shot at which the audience has been able to absorb most of its information. If you wait too long for the cut, the shot begins to drag and get boring. If you cut too soon, most of the audience may miss the meaning and become confused. In the end, the meaning of the commercial is intended to be attached to the brand. Therefore, somewhere in the flow of the commercial there should be one clear moment where an impression of the brand falls on the beat of the editing tempo. The Flow of Attention graph shows the visual "beats" from your audience's perspective and reveals whether or not the brand is on one.

Repetition: Use repetition to strengthen branding

While in our view an important factor in determining branding is that a brand impression occur at least once in a clear focal point of viewer attention, it is true that simple repetition of the brand can improve memorability and therefore, the branding process. If you accept the notion that repetition is useful in a particular commercial, then the question becomes, "How many times should the brand identity be repeated?" As an opinion, let us suggest the rule of three. The logic for this is the same as the logic for using three vignettes per commercial. That is, once is a curiosity, twice is a coincidence, and three times begins to form a pattern. In the example below, these three frames appeared at different times during one ad. The advertiser used repetition to strengthen branding.

Repeating brand shots in an ad is one way to improve branding.

This also fits with the ideas of the respected advertising researcher Krugman who believed that, from a media buying standpoint, three exposures are needed to optimize the impact of a television commercial. He argued that the three exposures correspond to three questions that are subconsciously asked by the television viewer: 1st exposure: What *is* it? 2nd exposure: What *about* it? 3rd exposure: What *of* it?

Brand Identifiers: Identify the brand in a variety of ways.

To get good Brand Linkage in your advertising, it is necessary to focus the viewer's attention on a strong brand impression. This does not necessarily mean the brand has to be identified only by the brand name. One of the advantages that well-established brands have is that multiple ways of identifying the brand have been built up by advertising over time in the form of "advertising equities." For example, soon after it was introduced in IBM advertising, the "blue letterbox" became a telegraphic cue to the target audience that they were watching an IBM commercial. The following is a list of some different ways the identity of a brand might be cued in a television commercial:

• **Name:** This is, of course, the most straightforward way of identifying the brand. But for new products, or in some categories such as pharmaceuticals, names that are difficult to read or ambiguous in their pronunciation can be difficult to work with creatively.

• **Slogan:** Which brand tells you to *Just Do It*? Which high-tech giant offers you, *e-business on demand*? A well-known slogan is one way of contributing to the identification of the brand being advertised, as well as encapsulating an entire brand positioning.

• **Symbols:** Which brand is identified by the symbol of the golden arches? Which telephone company is identified by the symbol of a pin dropping? A symbol or visual icon can become telegraphic cues to the identity of the brand being advertised. Some symbols can also become mnemonics, or memory aids, for encoding, in a highly compressed way, a fundamental promise of the brand. For example, the

Dove "milk drop shot" reminds consumers of Dove's heritage as a brand for healthy, soft skin.

• **Trade Characters:** Ownable brand characters such as the Snuggle Bear, Tony the Tiger, Mickey Mouse or the AFLAC duck.

• **Trade Dress:** Graphic elements that identify and therefore belong to the brand, such as the distinctive shapes of the Coca-Cola bottle or the Absolut vodka bottle, or in the soft drink category, the color red for Coke versus the color blue for Pepsi.

VII

Finding Ideas That Travel: What to look for in advertising global brands

VII

Finding Ideas That Travel: What to Look for in Advertising Global Brands

In broad terms, there are four potentially competing business objectives that must be kept in balance as a multinational corporation manages its international advertising.

• Brand Building by Speaking With One Voice

• Economies of Scale in Creative Production

• Maximizing Local Effectiveness

• Speed of Implementation

The main reason to do advertising at all is to build a brand. A global brand is one that stands for the same thing pretty much everywhere. While this does not necessarily require that identical advertising executions be used everywhere, it does require that the advertising communicates the same *meaning*, in terms of strategic messages and brand values, everywhere. In short, the brand needs to speak with *one voice*.

Advertising has to operate within given financial constraints. In general money saved in the cost of producing advertising executions can be put toward media buys to ensure that target audiences actually get an opportunity to see the advertising. The second objective, therefore, is to achieve *economies of scale* in the cost of creative production by re-using the same executions with minimal changes from one country to another. On the surface, this objective appears to line up with the first—in reality, as I have seen in our global pre-testing business, the same execution can work differently in different countries.

The most efficient advertising is advertising that makes each member of the target audience feel like the commercial is a personalized message sent directly to them. This is advertising the target audience is most likely to pay attention to, most likely to find relevant and emotionally engaging, and most likely to act on. Advertising that is developed in-country may have a home-court advantage in terms of how it scores on measures of performance—though we have seen that this is not always the case. The challenge of managing international advertising is to make the correct trade-offs between *in-country* customization versus *cross-country* efficiency.

Finally, the world of business is increasingly moving at internet speed. Projecting ideas around the world rapidly is one of the keys to winning the global "street fight" for new business.

CREATIVE OPTIONS

From a creative standpoint, there are three fundamentally different approaches to the development of advertising execution that we have seen used with varying degrees of success. These are importing executions, local production and importing ideas.

Importing Executions

Commercials are produced in one country and imported by other countries for use in their local markets. The logic of this strategy is two-fold. First, economies of scale are created by only having to produce one execution that can be used in multiple markets around the world. Second, and perhaps more important, the company can speak with one voice and project a consistent brand image around the world, hopefully leading to the creation of a global brand image.

The risks associated with this "one size fits all" approach arise from the fact that not all advertising can be expected to work equally well from one country to another. Failure can take various forms; advertising imported from one country to another can backfire by running afoul of cultural sensitivities in a foreign country. Trying to develop politically correct executions that work everywhere can lead to bland advertising that does not maximize local effectiveness, and third, an American-centric approach reminds one of the famous New Yorker's View of the World cartoon. Such ethnocentric uniformity ultimately can lead to a loss of perspective on the constantly changing world of opportunities facing the brand. At the very least, with an import strategy, a certain symmetry should apply. An execution that has been found to work very well in a foreign market should be a candidate for re-execution in the US market.

Local Production

The commercials produced are entirely unique to the country in which they are aired. The logic of this local "empowerment" strategy is that the in-country manager is closest to the market and therefore is most likely to be aware of cultural nuances and market conditions. In theory this leads to advertising with maximum local effectiveness.

In reality, the risk of this strategy is that the brand identity becomes fractured throughout the various markets; a result that is fundamentally at odds with the goal of a global brand. Local production also fails to create an economy of scale for creative production.

Importing Ideas

It is the *idea* behind an execution that gives it its meaning. If the goal of building a global brand is to make the brand stand for the same thing around the world then customers and potential customers everywhere should associate the same ideas with the brand. An execution and an idea are not the same thing; the movies *Seven Samurai* and *The Magnificent Seven* are the same story idea executed with a local cast for a Japanese and an American audience, respectively. In other words, there is a third strategy for managing global advertising.

Finding ideas that work globally—i.e. "ideas that travel"—is often the best strategy for achieving a balance in all four business objectives. First, using the same idea globally is a way of speaking with one voice. Second, finding good ideas is a significant part of the cost of creative development and can contribute to economies of scale in executing effective advertising ideas. Third, re-executing in a local market is a way of making sure that the idea has maximum appeal to the local market. Fourth, focusing management attention on rapidly deploying a single idea globally allows the modern brand to operate at internet speed—a new requirement for doing business globally.

Barriers To Universal Advertising

There are two fundamental reasons why an ad that performs well in one country may not perform as strongly in another. The first is based on executional considerations. Many of the details that go into making an effective execution may be fairly localized in their effects. A joke that is funny in one country may be offensive in another. A celebrity in one country may be completely unknown in another. If those kinds of factors appear to be central to the execution, so that taking them out fundamentally changes the commercial, then chances are you do not have a big, or global, advertising idea. A checklist of many of the executional variables that will affect how well your idea travels is shown at the end of this section.

The second reason that ads may not travel well is strategic. Obviously, a brands' positioning is defined with reference to its competitive set. The *competitive set*, and the brand's position within that set, may vary as a function of geography—e.g. you might be a market leader in one country, a minor player in another. Therefore, commercials designed to communicate strategic messages that reinforce a particular positioning can be expected to vary in performance internationally as a function of differences in the market context.

Keys to International Advertising: What We Have Learned

The Heuristic Model of Advertising is Global. Analysis of an extensive international pretesting database reported to the ESOMAR conference in Rome in 2001 validated with international data all the key relationships in the TV Advertising model presented at the front of this book.

What we found is that regardless of whether or not you are airing it in the US, Europe, South America or Asia/Pacific, an effective commercial can be defined as one that gets the Attention of its target audience, makes an impression of the Brand, and Motivates interest in doing business with the company. Moreover, regardless of which country you are talking about, the kinds of executions that get the attention of the audience are those that reward the viewer for the thirty seconds of time you are asking them to give you—by entertaining them, doing something they like, something that's different from anything else they've seen before. And regardless of which country, the way to motivate an audience is to communicate a relevant, believable, and brand-differentiating selling proposition in an emotionally dramatic way.

In other words, by validating the model with international data, it is clear that there is no need to re-invent in each country the research methods that have been developed for bringing discipline to the advertising process. Thus, while it may not be possible to always create universal commercial executions for global brand building, ad researchers can apply the same theoretical constructs for monitoring global advertising effectiveness.

What Has Worked

Brand image is determined with reference to the *self*—the "I" of the customer. A product has truly become a brand when it becomes "my product." The warmth and intimacy of the brand relationship is created in a variety of ways, from real experiences with the company to *virtual experiences* created by advertising. In fact, the "stories" that the best advertisers of global brands tell in their advertising does just that. This is in striking contrast to the kind of advertising that many business-to-business advertisers have been putting on air—a lot of computer graphics, montage, little narrative structure, emotionally bland.

In a content analysis of several hundred business to business commercials tested around the world we found that the following types of executions are superior in terms of their ability to attract the attention of the target audience:

- Focus on one idea
- From the customer point of view

- Utilizing humor
- Or Drama
- With lots of structure—i.e. stories
- Using characters
- In well-defined roles
- Dealing with problems of today (not the future)

Advertising that focuses on ideas or universal stories dealing with real human values, pays off in the long run compared to flashy video "technique" oriented ads that characterize so much business to business advertising. The challenge, however, is to generate this kind of advertising in a form that speaks to audiences around the world. In other words, it requires genuine insight into the human experience.

INTERNATIONAL BARRIERS TO EXECUTIONAL EFFECTIVENESS

These are some executional variables that can affect how well a particular execution translates from one country to another.

1. Complex Language Ads that are heavy on copy or highly abstract verbal ideas are not likely to travel well. Ads with stand up presenters are likely to fall into this category.

2. Dialogue Does the dialogue carry the story or do the visuals? A good way to consider this question is in silent film terms. The more the story can be conveyed visually, the more likely the execution will translate. Dialogue heavy stories require extensive subtitles which can impede the viewer's ability to process information quickly.

3. Ethnic Characters There are clearly biases in many countries against members of other races or ethnic groups. Sensitivity to these issues is clearly called for in developing global executions.

4. Local Celebrities For executions that use a celebrity it's important to gauge the limits of their fame. For example, television stars are less likely than movie stars to be international celebrities.

5. Business Roles Different cultures conduct business in different ways and so the casting of business roles may not always translate well. For example, showing a female manager in charge may not play as well in countries where women have not risen in management ranks as much as they have in the US.

6. Culturally Inappropriate Cues Props or other objects in the execution may take on unexpected meanings in other cultures.

7. Local Settings Unless it is intentional, it probably does not help to have "made in the USA" stamped all over the execution.

8. Humor Visual or slapstick humor is likely to travel better than humor based on wordplay.

9. Music Music tastes vary widely and musical trends travel around the world at different rates. Therefore, music-driven executions may test differently from one country to another.

VIII

5 Research Strategies for Improving Advertising Productivity

Reprinted from *Admap*, February 2005.

VIII

5 Research Strategies
for Improving Advertising
Productivity

Like the children of Lake Wobegon, all advertising ideas are above average—if you believe
the spin. But the statistical reality of the bell-
shaped curve is that only thirty out of every
one hundred ads you test will score above
average. Forty out of a hundred must, at least
the first time you test them, score only average.

No business wants to spend money on
average advertising. Competitive advantage is
gained in the marketplace only when you put
your money behind advertising that is superior
to your competitor's. But all too often, because
of the tyranny of the calendar and the need to
put something on air when the deadline of an
air date arrives, your advertising manager must
confront the reality of spending millions of
dollars on what is no more than an average
performer.

Advertising is the business process by which
ordinary products are made famous and turned
into stars. Unilever is a master of this process.
It markets over four hundred consumer brands

globally and last year spent $3.3 billion advertising them. Like the Hollywood dream factories of yesteryear, Unilever manufactures miniature movies world wide by the hundreds, each at a cost in the US rapidly approaching four hundred thousand dollars. And this is only the tip of the media iceberg. In the US, the industry rule-of-thumb is that while ten percent of the advertising budget is spent producing a commercial, ninety percent of the total budget is spent buying air time, which works out to nearly a five-million dollar investment associated with each and every television commercial.

How do you manage this expensive creative, and therefore frustratingly unpredictable process, to beat the averages? As shown in the model below, you can bring research discipline to the creative process by using five different learning strategies to repeatedly achieve productivity gains in advertising performance.

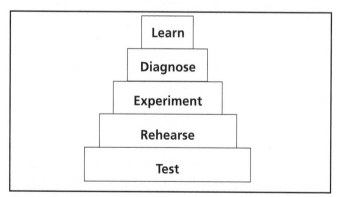

Five learning strategies for improving advertising productivity

1 ~ Test the advertising creative with a valid performance standard.

Who would launch a new product into a national marketplace without first testing it among consumers? It only makes sense to apply the same
logic to advertising, which is simply another
product of human ingenuity and craft. One way
of making sure that you are not putting money
behind average advertising is to set a firm performance standard that says an ad cannot go on
air unless it first achieves an above average
score in pre-testing research.

One of the secrets for identifying superior creative performers is making sure that you use
valid measures in the research—are the
measurements you collect actually related to
effectiveness in the marketplace? To answer
that question, advertising researchers have put
considerable effort and expense into getting the
research right.

Recently, Unilever stopped using day-after
recall testing in the US. A measure first popularized by P&G in the 1950s, day-after recall is still
the most widely-used commercial pre-testing
measure in the US. The impetus for the decision
to discontinue its use came out of research
(reported in Kastenholz, Young & Kerr, 2004)
comparing a sample of sixty commercials tested
in three different pre-testing systems. The
results showed that Recall scores systematically

rewarded boring, bland and emotionally uninvolving advertising.

Of course, this does not mean that you should stop using "hard" metrics to evaluate TV advertising. In place of Recall, Unilever uses a quantitative measure of breakthrough or attention-getting power; a measure that does not rely on an outdated and limited concept of how advertising enters the mind of the consumer. Modern research has shown that human memory is highly complex and involves several different systems in the brain. The type of memory that Recall testing taps into—semantic memory—is not, for example, the memory system where human emotional experience is recorded, which is known as the episodic system. So, like the joke about the drunk looking for his lost keys under the street lamp because that's where the light is, the historical preference for Recall testing may be a matter of looking in the wrong place for evidence of advertising effectiveness because that's where the research lights were shining in the past.

Changing the research performance standard to reward more experiential advertising, also improves the process of working with advertising agencies. As an artificial barrier to advertising creativity, Recall testing had for years been a great source of friction between Agency Creatives, Brand Managers and Researchers. Aligning the different stakeholders in the advertising development process with a common "mental model" of how advertising works, improves the vital collaboration between Creatives, Brand managers and Researchers.

2 ~ Rehearse the creative in rough form first.

What stand up comedian would take their act directly to a national television audience like the Tonight Show without trying out their jokes in a small nightclub first? Yet many advertisers go directly into final production of their expensive commercials without any kind of rehearsal in front of a real audience. As Senge (1990) points out in his book on learning organizations, *The Fifth Discipline*, "The almost total absence of meaningful 'practice' or 'rehearsal' is probably the predominant factor that keeps most management teams from being effective learning units."

For that reason, Unilever will test many advertising ideas at a rough stage of production first. Most television commercial concepts can be executed inexpensively in a cartoon form known as an "animatic", or with borrowed footage from other pieces of film in a form known as a "ripomatic." These rough versions cost only about a tenth as much as the final film and are usually good enough for testing purposes.

Rough production not only makes it cheaper to screen ideas, but it can also be used to make good ideas even better. Not all creative concepts are like the goddess Athena, who sprang fully-formed from the mind of Zeus. Sometimes a newborn idea has to come of age before being launched into the world.

In a review of fifty recent ad pre-tests, (Kastenholz, Young, & Dubitsky, 2005) compared the performance of commercials that went straight to final production, because of timing constraints or other reasons, with commercials that were first rehearsed in animatic form and then were fully produced with the creative benefit of research feedback. Ads that had been rehearsed first in rough production were + 28% stronger in terms of attention-getting power than those that skipped the rehearsal step and went straight to final film. What this means in financial terms is that we can spend less than $50,000 on the rough production and research of an advertising idea in order to make an approximately $1 million improvement in the audience impact of the final commercial. That's the value of rehearsal.

3 ~ Experiment with creative alternatives.

All babies are beautiful in the eyes of their parents. The same is true for creative concepts. To find the best solution to your advertising needs, you must avoid the trap of falling in love with your first idea.

One of the benefits of rough production,

therefore, is that it makes it cost-effective to test multiple options for an advertising campaign. Like new product development, creativity frequently boils down to a process of trial and error. Thomas Edison tried out over 3,000 different prototypes before hitting on the right way to make the electric light bulb.

According to the laws of statistics, if the first idea you test has a 30% chance of scoring above average, then testing two ideas gives you a 51% probability that one of them will score above average, testing three ideas gives you a 66% per cent chance, and testing four ideas gives you a 76% probability that at least one of your creative concepts will score above average on the first pass through the testing system. (This is based on the binomial distribution that arises from a series of Bernoulli trials.) For a new product launch, for example, where timetables are extremely tight and where you don't want to be forced into the position of launching with an average commercial for lack of better alternatives, it makes sense to plan in advance on testing multiple advertising concepts to gain favorable odds for success.

4 ~ Optimize the creative with diagnostic insights.
Remember, the first time through the testing system you can expect 4 out of every 10 ideas to score at an average level simply because of the laws of probability. Sometimes though, the

first execution of an idea produces a "diamond in the rough."

The ingoing assumption about pre-testing research is that many of the ideas that make it as far as the quantitative testing stage have the potential to be winners, but for some flaw in the execution that's holding them back. The primary goal of diagnostic research, therefore, is to help identify missed opportunities.

There's a huge gain in productivity to be realized if you can rework an idea that scores only average to make it into an above-average performer rather than throwing out the idea and starting over. Time as well as money is lost when you only use research as a filter for advertising ideas. The value of diagnostic pre-testing research, therefore, is optimization.

To begin with, diagnostic research is used to help the ad team answer the following question when confronted with a disappointing test score: Is this a little idea that has been well-executed, or is it a potentially big idea that has some executional flaw holding it back? Or in business terms, is this an idea worth investing additional time and money trying to fix?

For instance, some commercials Unilever has pre-tested score only at average levels on the performance measure of Attention, but score highly on diagnostic factors such as likability, originality or entertainment value—factors that normally are strongly predictive of above average attention-getting power. In those cases, look for some structural flaw in the flow of the film that might be fixed with a little re-editing. Think of it as the film equivalent of fixing a grammatical error in a sentence you is writing.

Next, the job of diagnostic research is to define the problem as precisely as possible—so that Creatives know what to fix! For that reason, don't just engage in copy-testing. Use both verbal and non-verbal diagnostic techniques to provide insights into how a commercial is performing. For example, the Ameritest Picture Sorts® technique allows us to understand how a commercial is working as a piece of film. These film direction diagnostics, the "Spielberg variables", are particularly important because, at the end of the day, the actionability of diagnostic advertising research can only be found in the editing room.

In a review of the hundred plus ads recently tested in a major Unilever business unit, fifty commercial executions were found, on the first pass through testing, to score only average on key performance measures—the normal rate we would expect from the Bell Curve. Diagnostics, however, suggested that half, or twenty-five, of these "average" commercials had untapped potential. So these commercials were re-edited based on the research findings.

As a quality control check, one in four had

been retested. And all but one of the executions improved significantly, from average to above average, on key measures—an 87% success rate for improving commercial performance among these underachievers.

In terms of both time and money, therefore, the overall contribution to advertising productivity can be substantial if you take an optimization approach to using research. Looking at the hundred plus ads produced by this business unit during the review period, nearly half, or 43%, of the of the ads that were approved for airing were first re-edited, or optimized, based on research findings. The following chart illustrates how diagnostic research provided a way to save a large number of creative ideas that

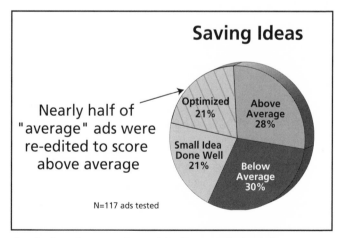

Optimize the creative with diagnostic insights

simply needed more polishing, while maintaining above average standards for performance.

5 ~ Learn from the competition.

From a benchmarking standpoint, it's not enough for your advertising to outscore the commercials averaged together in some historical norm base. The reality is that you have to beat the other guys' advertising—right now! Your advertised share-of-mind is not just a function of your share-of-voice, or ad spending, it's also a function of the relative strength of your advertising creative when compared to the competition.

Some years ago, Unilever had a run of weak test scores for one of their deodorant brands. This lead to much discussion about deodorant being a "low-involvement" category. It was theorized that deodorant test scores shouldn't be as high as in, say, the more glamorous shampoo category. To some, this line of explanation had the look and feel of a self-limiting mindset.

Then, a new marketing director who was a strong believer in research took over. He reasoned that the competition is selling the same kinds of products to the consumer in this so-called low-involvement category, so let's do some competitive intelligence and test some of their advertising to see their scores. Of course, the competition's advertising was found to significantly outscore his. With this new evidence, it wasn't long before his creative was scoring at this new higher level.

Competitive testing gives you a way of experimenting with different methods of reaching the consumer at someone else's expense. And if you have more powerful diagnostic tools for understanding why the consumer is responding the way she does to these different approaches, you may end up actually knowing more about your competitor's advertising than he does, and you learn how to beat him.

The new marketing director was responsible for a number of brands besides deodorant. From the beginning of his tenure, he began a program for systematically testing competitive advertising in all of his categories. What he learned from this competitive research found its way into the performance of his own advertising. When the average performance of ads produced during the two years prior to the onset of competitive ad testing was compared to the average performance of ads produced during the two years after competitive testing was done, in those same product categories, the Unilever average had increased by +19%.

Test, rehearse, experiment, diagnose, learn— that's the research mantra for improving advertising productivity. The chart below illustrates the performance of two hundred Unilever ads tested over a six-year period with this approach. A research system that simply filters advertising can raise or lower the hurdle for acceptable advertising performance, but it would not produce such a growth curve. This improvement in Unilever's advertising performance over time provides evidence for the effectiveness of working systematically with the strategies of test, rehearse, experiment, diagnose and learn.

Ameritest Performance Index for Unilever ads showing a learning effect.

IX

How to Have a Successful Research Meeting With The Ad Team

IX

How to Have a Successful Research Meeting With the Ad Team

When I heard the learn'd astronomer,
When the proofs, the figures, were ranged in columns
before me,
When I was shown the charts and diagrams, to add,
divide, and measure them,
When I sitting heard the astronomer where he lectured
with much
Applause in the lecture-room,
How soon unaccountable I became tired and sick,
Till rising and gliding out I wander'd off by myself,
In the mystical moist night-air, and from time to time,
Look'd up in perfect silence at the stars.
                                        —Walt Whitman

Walt certainly knew what it was like to be a Creative, even if he never sat in a conference room listening to the research report. But not being a businessman, he might not have understood that creating stars out of ordinary products and services requires that the successful marketing manager must find ways to get the poet and the scientist to communicate effectively with each another.

This has never been more important than now, when senior management is demanding on behalf of the board of directors "figures, ranged in columns" proving the return on investment before your advertising budget gets approved.

Many bright researchers have been working hard on behalf of advertising managers and their agencies on the messy problem of how to improve the accuracy of advertising measurement, particularly in that emotionally charged arena of advertising research known as "pre-testing" or "copytesting." Knowing *in advance* that you have a piece of advertising creative that will return a multiple of the ad spend to the bottom line is much more useful than learning after the fact from tracking studies that, unfortunately, last year's advertising (from the previous agency) didn't work.

Researchers have tried out different measures for predicting advertising performance: recall, persuasion, attention-getting power, likability, communication and so on. All of these have been found to be somewhat valid up to a point and therefore important, but none of them have been found to be perfect. So one of the conclusions that many of us researchers have painstakingly arrived at is what Creatives have been saying all along—that different ads can work in different ways and that there is no one simple formula for creating effective advertising.

Without getting into a debate about the pros and cons of different research measures, one of the overlooked implications of this conclusion is that for research to be a useful contributor to the process of developing effective advertising, Creatives must make the effort to communicate to the researcher how *their particular piece of creative is supposed to work*. Only then can the appropriate research methods be deployed, and the appropriate interpretations of the data given, to properly understand whether or not your advertising is, in fact, working as intended. In other words, Research and Creative folks must collaborate with one another!

WHAT ARE THE BARRIERS TO SUCCESSFUL COLLABORATION?

In a word, *emotions.*

Let's look at the range of emotions that are likely to accompany various findings on ads that you will be researching. In general, if you test enough ads over time, the results, regardless of which research system is used, will follow a bell-shaped curve, as shown in the chart on the following page. Ads that score in the top thirty per cent of ads tested will be described as "above average," which will undoubtedly be cause for

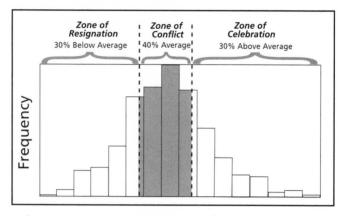

Ad test scores generate a range of emotions.

great celebration. Time to pop the champagne corks! The advertising manager, the agency, everybody—including the researchers—all look brilliant!

Ads that score in the bottom thirty percent of ads tested, unfortunately, will be described as "below average." This is, of course, cause for disappointment. Bad luck! Good try! But generally, if the research results are clear-cut in their meaning, most professionals will simply accept the verdict of the audience and move on to another idea. Emotionally, this is a *Zone of Resignation.*

The difficulty arises in the middle ground, the situation where the ad that was tested is described as only "average" or "at norm" statistically. Now, no one wants to be considered *average*, with its unspoken connotation of "mediocre." No ad manager wants to spend millions of marketing dollars behind an average advertising execution. At best, average advertising can be expected to cancel out competitive advertising, but it cannot be expected to grow the business substantially. There is no end-of-year bonus in that performance.

And yet, the research report isn't quite saying that the ad is "good" or "bad"—research reports are cautiously ambivalent about this. Perhaps it is only telling you that the work isn't quite done, that the creative execution needs a bit more polishing before its full potential is released. In this limbo state of average, there is a great deal of room for interpretation and for the various advocates of the ad in question to spin the data—or to question the limitations of the research methodology. But, given the tyrannical pressures of the marketing calendar, there is also a great need for the advertising team to understand what to do next.

Emotionally, when research has to report average scores for an advertising test you are now in the *Zone of Conflict*. Unfortunately, according to the laws of statistics, you will find yourself in this emotionally-charged situation about forty percent of the time.

How you deal with the complex emotional dynamics of this situation will determine whether or not you have a successful research meeting with the ad team. And no matter how excellent the research was from a technical or methodological standpoint, the advertising research project is not finished until you've had a successful meeting with the ad team. It is only when research is actually listened to that it can make a useful contribution to the creative development process.

One common mistake in managing the emotions present in the room is to pretend that they do not exist. A research meeting is not a court of law where the advertising is on trial and the judge admonishes the jury to set aside their emotions and look reasonably at the facts of the case. We have long believed that the dichotomy between reason and emotion is a false one in advertising. Thought and emotion work together in creating effective advertising. Therefore, the separation of these two human faculties is equally wrong when research is used to evaluate advertising effectiveness.

Great work comes from people who are passionate about their advertising ideas—so how could we possibly expect the ad team members to be dispassionate about the research findings on their work? In our experience, one of the most reliable indicators that the ad team is learning from the research is the visible conflict of ideas—as long as that conflict is productive and not taken to a personal level.

Another barrier to the successful research meeting is the college lecture-room format of most research presentations. Whitman has already warned us of the likely response to that style of delivery from agency Creatives. A sure sign of impending failure of the meeting is when the researcher assumes the role of expert professor and the ad team obligingly begins to ask questions about the research methodology, to take attention off the true, and in this case uncomfortable, subject of the meeting, which is the performance of the advertising.

GROUP INTERACTION: DIALOGUE IS THE HEART OF GROUP LEARNING

A sign of impending success is when everyone in the room is fully engaged in a lively give and take of ideas as the group struggles to understand the significance of the research reporting on the audience response to the advertising. Each person in the room should participate fully in the discussion with the goal of understanding and insight, not in winning points or attempting to make a particular preconceived point of view prevail.

This kind of group interaction is what Peter Senge describes in his management book on learning organizations, *The Fifth Discipline,* when he talks about dialogue as being at the heart of group learning:

> *"The purpose of dialogue is to go beyond any one individual's understanding. In dialogue, groups explore complex issues from many points of*

view. In dialogue, individuals gain insights that
simply could not be achieved individually."

Senge borrowed this idea from the late British physicist David Bohm, who wrote an insightful little book on the subject called *On Dialogue*. According to Bohm, the concept of "dialogue" is concerned with:

> *"...a stream of meaning flowing among and through us and between us. This will make possible a flow of meaning in the whole group, out of which may emerge some new understanding. It's something new, which may not have been in the starting point at all. It's something creative."*

THE ROLES IN THE MEETING: UNDERSTANDING THE EMOTIONAL DYNAMICS IN THE ROOM

Dialogue, then, should be focused on logos or meaning, not analysis. It should reflect the fact that people come from different backgrounds and experiences, with different opinions, assumptions and mental models about how things work. Collectively, then, we are able to explore the complex issues of advertising from many points of view.

Indeed, many points of view are represented in the typical advertising research meeting. For the purpose of understanding the emotional dynamics present in the room, it is useful to review the different positions within the organizations that are likely to be represented in the meeting, as diagrammed below.

Roles in the ad research meeting.

From the client side, three types of principal players might be present in the room, in addition to various assistants and observers. The first would be the senior marketing person in the room, such as the Marketing Director, who ultimately "owns" the brand and, therefore, would be the one who controls the advertising budget. The second would be the person charged with the day-to-day management of the brand and therefore, the one responsible for the development of strategy for the brand's advertising—the Brand Manager or Advertising Manager. The third important player in the room would be the primary client researcher on this piece of business, or these days, the "Consumer Insights Manager"—a title designed to reinforce the organizational emphasis on finding insights or the meaning of the research, and not just the collection and dissemination of data. This person, who is the research supplier's client, is responsible for the research contribution to the creative development process and therefore, in a very real sense, is the one who "owns the meeting."

From the agency side, there might be as many as four types of players present. First would be the Creative Director, who is the principal architect of the brand's advertising over time and, by virtue of her talent, knowledge and experience, occupies the position of the "advertising expert" in the room. Second would be the Creatives, typically teams of writers and art directors, who actually came up with the advertising concepts being tested. Third would be the Account Manager on the business who is responsible for managing the business relationships with the client and for interfacing day to day with the Creatives. Fourth, a key agency player these days is the Account Planner, whose job is to build bridges between consumer needs and desires and creative inspiration, which in the context of this meeting may mean filling the role of "translator" between the science of research and the art of advertising.

Finally, the research supplier might be in the room to present the research findings and facilitate the discussion—or this role might be assumed by the client researcher instead.

An emotional sensitivity to the different

viewpoints in the room is critical to the creation of a successful dialogue. This is not the same as deference to hierarchy. As Bohm points out, "Hierarchy is antithetical to dialogue, and it is difficult to escape hierarchy in organizations." If the senior person is used to having her views prevail because of her position, then successful dialogue will not occur. If junior people are used to withholding their views because of insecurity, then dialogue will also fail. For successful dialogue to take place, all players must participate fully, though that does not mean that all must agree.

What, then, are some of the differences in the roles that the different players positioned in the room can be expected to perform? We conducted group discussions among client and agency personnel on the subject of how to have a successful research meeting. This is what they suggested.

The **Marketing Director** is the decision maker in the room and therefore her primary job is to actively listen rather than talk. If she makes her views known too early, she is likely to create a situation of "follow the leader," which is counterproductive to the purpose of dialogue. That being said, she does have a role at the beginning of the meeting to validate the objectives of the advertising. Since her business goals are at stake she should also clearly challenge the group for excellence and make it clear that she holds the work to the highest standards. Finally, at the end of the meeting she should take the responsibility to sum up learnings. This is important so that the group understands what she has internalized from the research findings that will affect her decision-making. She should set next steps so that the actions to be taken as a result of the research are clear to everyone and that the group can move forward.

The **Brand Manager/Advertising Manager** should provide the "set-up" for the meeting by reminding the group of the brand strategy and the objectives the creative is designed to achieve. As the "advertising buyer" on behalf of the company, the Brand Manager should be disciplined in examining the research to be sure that the advertising has met those objectives. But in performing the role of buyer-critic, it should be clear that all comments reflect a critique of the *work* with an eye toward identifying opportunities for improvement, and not criticisms of the people doing the work. A key role of the brand manger/ad manager is motivational; to be a cheerleader in order to get the best possible work out of the team.

The **Consumer Insights Manager/Client Researcher** validates the methodology through her endorsement and makes sure that the meeting is spent discussing what is important, namely the advertising, and does not degenerate into a confusing discussion of methodological minutiae. Her job is to help explain and clarify the research findings in order to illuminate the meaning of the research to the other team members. If there is a problem with the performance of the advertising execution, her job is not to tell the Creatives how to solve the problem but rather is to *define the problem as precisely as possible* so that that the Creative Team can focus on coming up with appropriate solutions.

The **Creative Director** is the primary source of advertising expertise in the room and therefore should provide relevant mental models and examples for framing the discussion of the creative issues. This means providing a "big-picture" view of how a particular execution fits the client's objectives for the brand. The Creative Director should also set a positive tone for the meeting by signaling an interest in the consumer's response to the advertising, actively taking the lead by discussing the research findings.

The **Creatives** are in the most emotionally vulnerable and uncomfortable of positions, for it is their work that is being publicly critiqued. Simply being there to listen and learn signals their willingness to stand behind the quality of their work and their genuine interest in the success of their clients. As painful as it is, whenever a gap opens between the creative intent of the execution and the audience response to the execution, this represents an opportunity to learn a new insight about the consumer to whom they are trying to sell. As seekers of missed opportunities, Creatives should actively participate in the discussion and not sit quietly in the room. By far, the best research meetings are those where the Creatives do much of the talking.

The **Account Director** is the strategic partner of the Brand Manager and therefore the co-creator of the strategy. As the organizing hub of the agency resources her job is to keep the discourse grounded in the practicalities of keeping the advertising process on its timetable and within budget. But on an emotional level, her job is to provide moral support to the vulnerable creative spirit so as to encourage risk-taking and the inevitable missteps that are implicit in creating outstanding work. In research meetings, she will frequently come across as the "defender" of the work, championing ideas in order to provide the emotional momentum necessary to get an idea through to completion.

The **Account Planner** bridges the worlds of science and art by helping to interpret and translate the research findings in ways that the Creatives find helpful. Since creative inspiration is frequently an intuitive or "inner-directed" process, the planner provides a counterpoint by bringing an "outer-directed" focus on the consumer, much like research, but typically with a more conceptual rather than technical orientation.

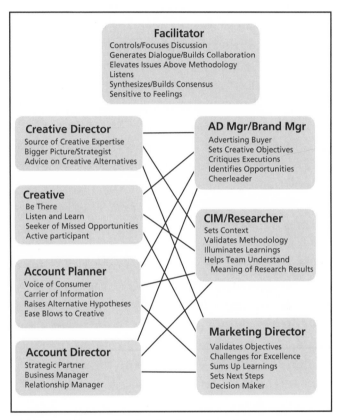

Relationships and roles in the advertising research meeting.

THE THREE CONDITIONS NECESSARY FOR DISCOURSE

Because advertising development is inherently a collaborative process, these roles will all tend to overlap. But it's important for understanding the emotional dynamics of the group inter-action to understand the differences in view-points of the various stakeholders at the start of the meeting.

According to Bohm, three conditions are necessary for discourse:

1. All participants must "suspend" their ingoing assumptions and preconceptions;

2. All participants must regard one another as colleagues;

3. There must be a facilitator who holds the "context."

Conversely, the absence of these conditions will tend to undermine the successful outcome of the meeting. Regarding the first point, if participants take a "defensive" stance in the meeting, arguing from their fixed preconceptions, even in the face of research findings, their minds are closed to learning and the meeting will not accomplish anything useful. True learning occurs when you confront the gap between assumptions or expectations and reality. According to an old adage in business, it isn't what you don't know that leads to failure, it's what *you think you know that isn't true.*

The second point is a matter of trust. If one party doesn't trust the others to interpret the data correctly or draw the "right" conclusions, this will lead to attempts to control or spin the research findings. This represents a fundamental lack of respect for your colleagues that will, again, undermine the ability of the team to learn as a whole. Respect for differences in viewpoint and trust in the good intentions of all present are fundamental to creative collaboration. Bohm points out the importance of taking the correct emotional stance in the meeting:

> *"We have been saying that people in any group will bring to it their assumptions, and as the group continues meeting those assumptions will come up. Then what is called for is to suspend those assumptions, so that you neither carry them out nor suppress them. You don't believe them, nor do you disbelieve them; you don't judge them as good or bad. Normally when you are angry you start to react outwardly and you may just say something nasty. Now suppose I try to suspend that reaction. Not only will I now not insult that person outwardly, but I will suspend the insult I make inside of me. Even if I don't insult somebody outwardly, I am insulting him inside. So I will suspend that, too."*

Third, it is important that a facilitator be present to empower the different members of the group to express their views freely and to keep the discussion focused on how the advertising is working. Indeed, the skills needed to generate true discourse in a research meeting with the ad team are really no different from the skills a focus group moderator brings to the business of generating insights from a group of consumers who have never met each other before. Admittedly, it's rare to find internal business meetings run as well as focus groups.

It is difficult for the Client Researcher or Consumer Insights Manager to play the role of moderator because of their need to be perceived as a member of the team, that is, as someone who is herself ego-invested in the success of the advertising. A mistake that Client Researchers sometimes make is to present themselves as somehow *objective* and therefore somehow indifferent to whether or not the research findings are positive or negative. Nothing could be further from the truth. There is a great difference between objectivity and the willingness to suspend your assumptions about the nature of reality. The Client Researcher cares as much as any other member of the ad team about developing winning advertising, and this must be communicated emotionally to the other members of the ad team in order to be accepted as a valued counselor. For that reason, the Client Researcher will often allow the supplier to play the role of facilitator, particularly when the results are controversial or negative.

As previously noted, the facilitator's role is not so different from that of a skilled focus group moderator, though, of course, she may also have to be able to answer questions of a technical nature about the quantitative research methodology that was used. In general, the facilitator must control or focus the discussion. In particular, she should elevate the issues above the methodology and keep them focused on the advertising. She should generate dialogue and build collaboration by actively listening, being sensitive to feelings and the emotional dynamics of the group, and by helping to synthesize the different threads of thought in order to build consensus around the meaning of the research.

The facilitator must be aware of the temptation to take the stage and focus the spotlight of attention on herself, to play the role of "expert." Shrewd advice to Facilitators is that, like the character played by Peter Sellers in the movie *Being There*, the more the other people in the group talk, the smarter you seem to get.

CAUSES OF FAILURE AND SUCCESS IN A RESEARCH MEETING

To sum up, then, what are the sources of failure in a research meeting with the ad team? Here are some of the big ones:

▼ Lack of agreement on objectives
▼ Data is confusing/contradictory
▼ Research findings are seen as "black box" without face validity
▼ Discussion is focused on the methodology rather than the advertising
▼ Emotional dissonance
  - Creatives feeling attacked
  - Creatives feeling like they are being told what to do
  - Not knowing what to do as a next step
▼ Researcher comes across as a know-it-all or as too academic
▼ Researcher tries to "play creative director"
▼ The researcher lectures the ad team, rather than generating discussion.

How do you know if you've actually had a successful meeting with the ad team? If the members of the ad team report the following positive experience:

▲ Everyone talked, particularly Creatives
▲ All points of view were heard
▲ Focus is on learning, not report card results
▲ Positive emotions were created

▲ Clear understanding of how ad worked
▲ Clear understanding of opportunities for
improvement
▲ Clear understanding of next steps.

In short, a successful research meeting means your ad team has received a communication back from their target audience and the gap, if it exists, between creative intent and audience response has been explored fully. In that case, the *Zone of Conflict* has become the *Zone of Opportunity*.

X
How To Talk The Talk: Glossary of Advertising Research Terms

X

How To Talk The Talk: Glossary of Advertising Research Terms

Action Standard
The minimum acceptable performance on key measures for an ad to qualify for airing. An Action Standard is not a single Hurdle Rate or a Norm to exceed, but may consist of several measures to meet or beat, singly or in combination.

Aesthetic Emotion
As defined by Aristotle, this is the kind of emotion produced by works of art where thought and emotion come together. Aesthetic emotion—also known as "working emotion"— is the key to building consumer relationships with a brand.

AIDA Model of Advertising Effectiveness:
This is one of several "hierarchy of effects" models that describes how advertising works.

In a nutshell, this model says that consumers pass through several stages in a certain order on their journey from prospects to customers. The first step is *Awareness* of the product or service. As the prospect gathers more information, this awareness becomes *Interest*. Then, over time, the interest morphs into *Desire* or a preference. And, finally, the desire (or Motivation) leads to *Action* (or actual purchase behavior). Critics of this approach point out that it isn't relevant to impulse purchasing (which follows an "awareness-action-desire" pattern).

Animatic

An inexpensive, cartoon-like rendering of a commercial concept for testing purposes that lacks the high production values of finished film. Testing animatics, instead of finished film, reduces the cost of testing multiple advertising concepts in order to identify winners. It provides creatives with the opportunity to rehearse their idea so it can be optimized in

Animatic Frame   *Finished Film Frame*

final production. This category also includes ripomatics, stealomatics, and photomatics.

Archetype

This is an elementary idea or feeling that has "deep meaning," occurs in all societies, and is readily understood. The great psychologist Carl Jung created this notion of archetype after observing the underlying themes and commonalities of myths across cultures. From a brand-building standpoint, archetypes are used to position a brand, serve as building blocks for brand persona/identity, and inspire brand imagery for creative development. Examples from the marketing realm would be the Jolly Green Giant (based on the pagan "Green Man," who symbolized fertility and abundance) and the Marlboro Man (an icon of masculinity, freedom, and independence).

Attention

This is one of the earliest perceptual/cognitive stages in processing stimuli that we are alerted to from any of our five senses. Attention occurs when we decide to tune in to certain stimuli for further processing in short-term memory, thereby tuning out other stimuli. In the 1890s, the great psychologist William James defined attention as "the focalization of consciousness"; a process to help one make sense out of the "blooming, buzzing confusion" experience of the world. In contrast, modern psychologists conceptualize attention in terms of processing capacity, resource allocation, and time-sharing.

Awareness

A measure of a respondent's conscious knowledge. Ad awareness is usually measured in tracking studies (either telephone or online) after advertising has run in the market. Usually, separate measures of unaided (spontaneous), aided (prompted), and top-of-mind awareness are collected in ad tracking studies. For example, Top of Mind Awareness refers to the percent of respondents who mention a given brand as the first one in response to an unaided brand awareness question. This relates to the concept of brand "salience."

Banner

All of the columns that run across the top of a page in a cross-tabulation. The industry standard is to include 16 to 18 points in a banner. For example, Gender consists of two banner points—Male and Female. There is typically more than one banner in a complete cross-tabulation job or "run." The banner points are usually the independent variables in a study.

Base

The number of respondents answering a particular question in a market research interview.

Bell Curve

Also known as the normal distribution or normal curve. Many variables tend to follow a bell curve, such as IQ, waist size, and pre-testing scores. This curve describes the values of a variable that have the following characteristics:

• Most of the values cluster about the average, with very few values extending way below the average and very few extending way above the average

• The distribution of values is symmetrical relative to the average

• Roughly 40% of all scores in a bell curve will be "average."

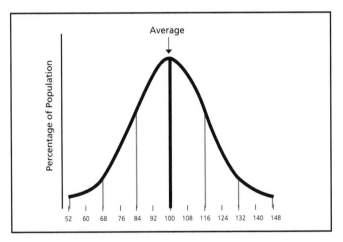

Example of a Bell curve.

Benefit

The concept of looking at a brand feature from the point of view of the customer. Basically, benefits answer questions such as, "Why would that be important to me?" For example, the benefits of a special ingredient in a new shampoo might be the consumer benefit of beauty. It is an old adage in marketing that consumers buy benefits, not features.

Brain Waves

A physiological approach measuring advertising effectiveness by examining the type of overall electrical activity of the brain (i.e., brain waves) through the use of an electroencephalograph (EEG).

Brand Attributes

The various aspects of product performance on which a target brand is likely to be evaluated by consumers versus a set of competitive alternatives. For a food product, brand attributes might include the concepts of taste and convenience. Usually ratings from ten to twenty features and benefits are collected in a pre-test. Differences across brand attribute ratings are used to assess the relative strengths and weaknesses of different commercials to position a brand within its competitive set.

Brand Image

The set of emotional and sensory inputs that a consumer associates with a particular brand in their episodic (i.e., emotional/ autobiographical) memory system. Popularized by ad legend David Ogilvy, this notion of brand image is complementary to brand positioning, which represents a brand's place within the semantic (rational) memory system. One of the principal ways advertising works is by building a distinctive image of a brand over time, which forms an emotional basis for brand loyalty.

Branding or Brand Linkage

The degree to which the recipient of the advertising understands that the commercial message was from the manufacturer or source of the product or service. From a quantitative standpoint, it is a measure of the strength of the linkage between the advertised message and the brand. Advertising with a very low level of brand linkage sells the product or service *category* rather than the *brand*.

Brand Stretch

In order to grow a brand, advertising needs to take creative risks to stretch consumers' perceptions of the brand, but not too far. Advertising that goes "too far" creates a disconnect between the brand and the consumer. Advertising that follows a "Goldilock's principle" and is "just right" has one foot in the past and one foot in the future.

Consumers have a new idea or feeling about the brand from watching the commercial. The brand has been successfully stretched in the mind of the consumer.

Just Right

Too Safe

Too Daring

Consumers don't learn or feel anything new about the brand.

Consumers don't feel the commercial fits the brand.

Brand Stretch

Branding Moment

Branding Moments are moments where thought and feeling come together in the ad. This is a theoretical concept put forward as a psychological mechanism for achieving long-term advertising effects. Branding Moments represent those peak moments in a television commercial, in both cognitive and emotional terms, when the advertising experience simultaneously enters both the episodic and semantic memory systems, thus linking both sides of the mind to the brand. These are the high points of aesthetic emotion where advertising imagery is given a clear meaning in terms of a brand's competitive positioning in the consumer's mind. Branding moments can be identified by plotting the Flow of Attention against the Flow of Emotion.

Thought and emotion come together to build the Brand Image for the long term.

CAPI

Computer Assisted Personal Interview. A PC is used to administer the survey to the respondent, and is controlled by the interviewer, who typically enters some or all of the respondent's input.

Cell

A research unit, sub-sample or group within a research study. For example, in a two-cell study, the first cell of respondents would be exposed to one ad while in the second cell, a different group of respondents would be exposed to a different ad.

Classification Variables

These are measures that relate to product/brand usage and lifestyle variables (as distinct from demographic variables). They are typically obtained at the end of a survey.

Click-Through Rate

The proportion of those exposed to a banner ad on the internet who actually click through on the ad to go to the connecting web page. These days, click-through rates are usually less than one percent.

Closed-Ended Questions

A question in a survey that requires the respondent to choose one or more pre-listed answers.

Coding

The process by which open-ended verbal responses are converted into numeric categories so that they can be tabulated. Verbal statements made by respondents in an interview are collected. The ideas they express are classified into groups according to meaning. The nets and subnets created by these groupings can be used quantitatively to measure how effectively a commercial communicates its intended messages. Generally, this is a subjective, interpretive exercise. Dialogue between client and researcher is usually needed to reach agreement on the content of the various categories for consumer language.

Cognitive Unconscious

This is *not* Freud's repository of idiosyncratic sexual and emotional symbols, but rather the mental processes that are operating outside the realm of awareness. These processes are brought to bear upon our perception and experience of the world. Some marketers have argued that we are *unaware* of as much as 95% of our cognitive processing.

Commercial Ratings

A set of statements used to assess reactions to the execution itself, rather than perceptions of the brand created by the advertising (i.e., brand attributes). These would include statements capturing such dimensions of commercial performance as likability, entertainment value, relevance of the message, believability and confusion. In a standard interview, a common core of rating statements is asked across all ad tests. There are also optional statements that address specific creative issues or areas of concern about a particular ad.

Communications Brief

Also known as Creative Brief. A one-page document produced by the advertising team to summarize the intended message take-away or emotional effects of the commercial on the target consumer. Briefs will usually contain background information on the target consumer, a reference to the consumer insight(s) that lead to this particular advertising idea, product claims to be made, supporting reasons to believe these claims, and other considerations.

Communications Strategy

Also known as Creative Strategy. The primary message take-away intended by the advertising team. The strategy is best expressed when focused on a single most important point to communicate, or the feeling that the consumer is supposed to take away after viewing the advertising. Getting the strategy right is half the job of developing effective advertising. It should be developed before the creation of advertising executions and is a key criteria for coding the respondent verbatims in the communication part of the pre-test.

Construct

Every field of inquiry, including market research, has theory and data. Theory refers to an explanatory framework that unifies key learnings from data, thereby providing understanding. A theory provides a connection between many separate elemental ideas or concepts. A technical name for an elemental idea or concept is a construct, or, more formally, a theoretical construct. For example, many pretesting systems subscribe to a theory that identifies Attention, Branding, and Motivation as key constructs that explain in-market purchase behavior. These constructs cannot be observed directly; they are defined by various measurement rules. Also called Theoretical Construct.

Continuous Advertising Tracking

This methodology gathers information on ad awareness, brand awareness, and brand perceptions through interviews that are conducted on a continuing basis. The key benefit is that responses can be examined for any particular time period—on a weekly, bimonthly, monthly, or quarterly basis—so that the impact of advertising flighting, sales promotions, or other marketing events can be lined up accurately with consumer responses. This approach is in marked contrast to the "wave" or "dipstick" method of advertising tracking, in which a limited number of interviews are conducted on a fixed monthly or quarterly basis. The downside of the wave or dipstick approach is that the timing of waves may inadvertently miss or fail to capture key marketing events.

Control Cell

A cell that receives no exposure to advertising, thus providing benchmark ratings of brand/service/product ratings which are compared against ad exposure cells to evaluate the impact of advertising.

Copy Sort

A parallel technique designed to complement the Picture Sorts technique to deconstruct the audience experience of a television commercial. The copy sort deals with words or copy rather than visual images. Three optional sorts may be used in sorting phrases and verbal ideas from the ad on the basis of 1) attention or recall, 2) relevance, or 3) feelings. Usually a five-point rating scale is used for sorts on relevance or feelings. In analysis, attention should be paid to both ends of the rating scale (e.g., top- and bottom-box ratings) in order to understand the dramatic impact of the language used in the commercial.

Correlation Coefficient

Also known as the Pearson Product-Moment Correlation Coefficient. Correlation is a measure of the relationship between two variables. It can indicate that as one variable increases in value, the other one decreases in value (showing an inverse or negative correlation). Alternatively, it can also indicate that as one variable increases in value, the other one also increases in value (showing a positive correlation). The numeric value of the correlation (i.e., the correlation coefficient) is a decimal that can range from plus one to minus one. The value of +1.00 represents a perfect positive correlation (the variables are synonymous), a value of -1.00 represents a perfect negative correlation (the variables are opposites), and a value of 0.00 represents a lack of correlation—the variables are independent. For example, height and weight are positively correlated in that people who are tall tend to weigh more than those who are short.

Day-After Recall Testing

A method of testing advertising effectiveness pioneered by Burke and still widely used in the US by systems such as Ipsos-ASI and ARS. The memorability of the advertising is measured by asking respondents to remember the advertising a day after it has been shown on television by using category and brand retrieval cues.

Demographic Variables

Variables that relate to the lifestage, age, gender, income, marital status, employment, educational level, occupation, and household structure of consumers.

Diagnostics

A set of verbal and non-verbal measures that are designed to provide insights and understanding into how an ad is working. (In contrast, evaluative measures are used to make a go/no go decision.) Diagnostic measures are used to explore gaps between creative intent and audience response. Diagnostic measures should be used to identify opportunities for improving executions that are performing poorly, and to explain the strengths of strong commercials so that future advertising development can build on that success. In general, diagnostic measures are used to gain insight into the pattern of results for evaluative measures. They tell you *why* rather than *what*.

Discontinuity in the Flow

This is a jarring or abrupt drop in audience attention to the visuals in the Flow of Attention graph. It suggests that the audience is momentarily confused by the film and is not tracking with the intended flow of images. Discontinuities should be examined to distinguish

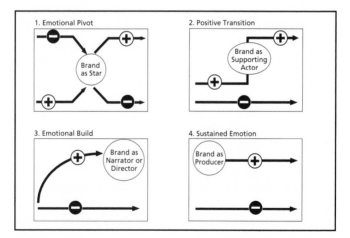

The four dramatic structures identifies with the Flow of Emotion®.

between trivial breaks due to fluidity in camera movement, and more critical breaks due to poorly executed transitions between key scenes. Discontinuities are also to be distinguished from the continuously smooth rising and falling curves that form the natural rhythms of the Flow of Attention. (See *Visual Connectedness* in this glossary.)

Dramatic Structure

The narrative structure of a piece of advertising film intended to create a particular emotional effect on the audience. It is distinct from lectures or rational sales presentations made to the consumer. Ameritest has identified four archetypal dramatic structures in advertising that can be analyzed with the Flow of Emotion: 1) Emotional Pivot, 2) Positive Transition, 3) Emotional Build, and 4) Sustained Emotion (all listed in this glossary). Recognizing gaps between the intended creative structure of an ad and the audience's actual emotional response is a major diagnostic for advertising performance.

Emotional Build

One of four archetypal dramatic structures identified with the Flow of Emotion. It is also known as Director-type advertising. This type of structure is characterized by a rising pattern in the positive Flow of Emotion as the viewer becomes more involved with the ad. It is sometimes associated with the reveal technique since the identity of the brand is generally withheld until the end of the commercial.

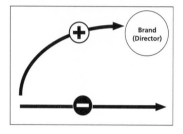

Emotional Pivot

One of four archetypal dramatic structures identified with the Flow of Emotion. It is also known as Star-type advertising. In this type of advertising, the commercial makes deliberate use of negative emotions early in the ad in order to establish emotional conflict or dramatic tension. The negative emotions are then turned into strong positive emotions with the arrival of the brand, which is the hero, or star, of the spot.

Emotional Structure

The intended emotional or affective response to a commercial that is analyzed with the Flow of Emotion.

Entry Point for the Eye

This is the area within a print ad that is first noticed by the reader and serves as a "hook" to draw her into the experience of the ad. Clear entry points are usually key to the Stopping Power or attention-getting power of print ads.

Episodic Memory

One of several human memory systems identified by Endel Tulving, a leading memory researcher and theorist in Cognitive Psychology. This is the system where personal memories are stored and the concept of self is located, in contrast to the Semantic memory system. The Episodic system is key to understanding the concept of Brand Image and the workings of experiential advertising, and is generally accessed through qualitative projective techniques and, quantitatively, by the Picture Sorts technique.

Esthetic Information

One of two types of information present in every piece of communication, in contrast to semantic information. Esthetic information is personalized as it relates to internal states of mind, and is associated with emotional or sensory content. It is not translatable from one channel of communication to another. It is the part of the picture that cannot be put into words—the poetry but not the semantic content of language. You could think of this as information about what you experience through your five senses and/or how you feel about these experiences. Also known as Aesthetic Information.

Executional Peak

A peak in the Flow of Attention that does not contain product-related content, such as a package shot, product in use, product demo etc. Executional peaks usually contain the emotional or aesthetic high points of the commercial narrative and are strongly linked to commercial enjoyment and attention-getting power.

Experiential Advertising

Advertising designed to associate a particular emotional or sensory experience with the brand as opposed to advertising designed to communicate rational selling propositions. Emotional advertising is a subset of this type of advertising as are commercials, such as appetizing food commercials, that are designed to evoke strong sensory responses from the audience. Experiential commercials create their strongest effects in the episodic memory system. Some researchers prefer to use the term experiential advertising rather than emotional advertising, because of the historical baggage associated with the latter.

Eyetracking

A technology that uses a camera to record how a reader's eye moves through the visual layout of a print ad or package design. This technology is not portable and, consequently, is often used during in-person interviews at a central-location facility.

Factor Analysis

A family of multivariate statistical procedures which use correlation analysis to reduce the number of variables in a set of rating scales. For example, factor analysis of a set of 30 rating statements might discover only 5 real, underlying dimensions (or *factors*) in the data.

As an illustration, "the ad is clever and quite entertaining" and "the ad was a lot of fun to watch and listen to" are correlated statements that are part of an "entertainment" factor.

Features

The functional attributes or dimensions of brand performance that consumers consider in making a choice among competitors in a given category. Communicating an important, believable brand differentiation feature can be a key rational component in developing highly motivating advertising.

Fieldwork

This is the data collection phase of a research study when respondent interviews are completed.

Fit

One of two factors (the other being "focus") that determine how well branded a commercial is. In a well-branded ad, the creative concept of the execution should be in character with or "fit" in with the underlying values of the brand.

Flow of Attention®

A proprietary technique developed by Ameritest that measures the moment-by-moment attention of the audience to the flow of visuals through a commercial. By sorting images from the ad based on visual recognition some time after exposure to the commercial, this technique deconstructs the cognitive processes of selective perception involved in the commercial viewing experience. This technique is a powerful diagnostic for the performance of the commercial in terms of Attention and Branding.

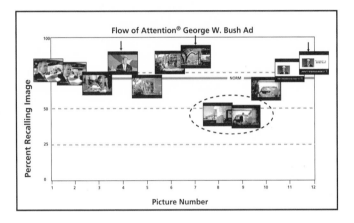

Flow of Emotion®

A proprietary technique developed by Ameritest that measures the moment-by-moment emotional response of an audience to the flow of visuals through a commercial. By sorting images from the ad on a feelings scale and examining the positive and negative responses to the images, this technique deconstructs the dramatic structure of the commercial in terms of affect or emotional response to the ad, rather than rational response to the messaging. This technique is a powerful diagnostic for the performance of the commercial in terms of Motivation.

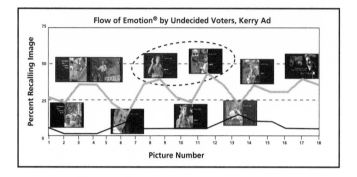

Flow of Meaning®

A proprietary technique developed by Ameritest that measures the moment-by-moment flow of meaning in the audience response to the visuals in a commercial. In this technique, images are sorted into a number of different categories of intended meanings, which are pre-determined from the Creative Brief. This is a powerful diagnostic for pinpointing the source of different brand values communicated by the advertising. See *Meaning of Images* in this glossary.

Frequency

A media measure which reports the *number of times* within a given time period that a proportion of your target audience is exposed to your advertising message. This is the companion concept to media *reach*. Conceptually, the concepts of reach and frequency account for the breadth and the depth of the advertising media buy, respectively.

Gross Rating Points (GRPs)

This represents the total *media weight* spent behind advertising, measured in terms of the number of households who have been exposed to the ad at least once and how many times they have seen it—i.e. reach and frequency. One GRP means one percent of households have seen the ad one time.

Heuristic Model

A teaching model designed to provide a road map to help business managers understand how to think about different measures collected in the Ameritest interview. It integrates advertising constructs and separates information vertically in terms of evaluative versus diagnostic variables, and horizontally in terms

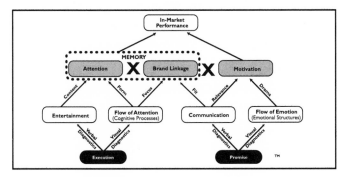

Ameritest heuristic ad model.

of executional versus strategic variables. It also shows how non-verbal picture sort variables complement traditional verbal measures.

Incentive

Payment to the respondent for taking the time to do an interview, usually either a small cash amount or the opportunity to win a larger prize in a lottery.

Incidence

This is the percent of the population who are in a given target group. For example, the incidence of male 21–24 year-old beer drinkers is 18%.

Index

A performance score generated by taking a raw measure from the interview and dividing it by the average performance on that measure from a particular database (e.g., an in-country database of ads tested) and then multiplying it by 100. An index of 100 means that an ad performs at an average level compared to ads from that particular database.

Key Metrics

The performance measures used to evaluate advertising in the go/no go decision.

Laddering

A qualitative technique used for uncovering the underlying values operating in a given category. The technique usually involves asking the simple question, "Why is that important to you?" over and over again as consumer responses ladder from brand features to consumer benefits to consumer values. For example, the consumer benefit of beauty in the skin care category might ladder up to the consumer value of self esteem.

Lifestage

From a pre-testing standpoint, product lifestage is generally divided into the two categories of new products and established brands. New product ads generally work quite differently from established brand ads. For example, creative briefs usually call for new product ads to be "introductory" in tone. Some suppliers make additional distinctions among established brands, such as "relaunch" for ads designed to "reposition" an established brand, or "power brands" for brands that totally dominate a given category.

Mall Intercept

A data collection technique in which the interviewer screens potential respondents from within a mall and, if they meet the screening criteria, brings them to a central location facility within the mall for interviewing.

Marketing Mix Modeling or Analysis

The marketing mix refers to factors within the marketer's control that ultimately satisfy the needs of customers. Some pundits call these factors the four Ps—*price, product* (which includes packaging or services), *promotion* (which includes any kind of marketing communication, such as advertising, sales promotions, PR, etc.), and *place* (anything related to distribution—getting the services or products to prospects and customers). From a business standpoint, marketing mix analysis describes the effects of these factors on one another and on sales volume. What is the incremental value of each of these elements of the marketing mix? Which of these elements returns the highest amount of profit to the corporation? How would you reallocate your budget to these various elements to optimize your return on investment? In a nutshell, this approach is used primarily for consumer packaged goods and requires advanced statistical analysis of sales data, spending data, and consumer response data.

Meaning of Images

Visual images are inherently ambiguous until the multiple possible interpretations of an image are collapsed into a single or dominant meaning by accompanying copy or by the context of placement in the story of the commercial. Determining whether or not a particular image in a commercial conveys appropriate meaning or brand value can be determined by a picture sort by having respondents sort images into different "buckets" of meaning. These results show the percent of respondents selecting a given concept as the one that best describes the image.

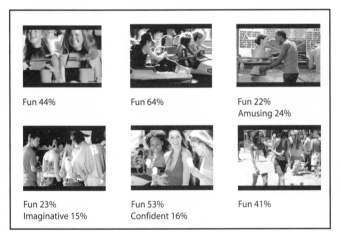

Data from a Flow of Meaning sort.

Metaphor

A general term encompassing many non-literal linguistic devices (e.g., analogy, simile) to communicate information. From a marketing standpoint, the metaphor is the royal road to the consumer's repository of unconscious thoughts about brands, products, and services. Projective techniques leverage metaphorical thinking to tap into these depths of knowledge.

Motivation or Persuasion:

Since the goal of advertising is to influence attitudes, intentions, and behaviors, motivation or persuasion is conceptualized as the final step in the decision-making process. Some modern theories suggest that there are two routes to effective persuasion. In a *central route*, consumers engage in careful and considerate rational processing that leads to a purchase decision. By contrast, in a *peripheral route*, consumers engage in what might appear to be impulsive decision-making based on positive or negative emotions in response to imagery, sounds, and language that are associ-

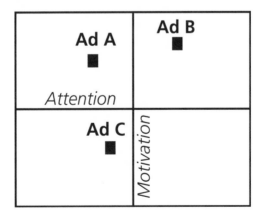

A graph of Attention vs. Motivation which are independent, or uncorrelated, variables.

ated with the advertising messages. Not surprisingly, most theories of persuasion emphasize either rational or emotional factors.

NAIC
North American Industrial Classification code. The US Bureau of the Census has updated what had previously been called SIC (Standard Industrial Classification) codes. This is a numerical system in which six-digit codes are used to represent all possible industries or types of businesses based on the products and services they provide. For a complete list in downloadable text file format go to http://www.census.gov/epcd/naics02/naicod02.txt

Nets
When coding verbal content from open-ended questions, a net counts people, not ideas. The net counts the actual number of respondents who play back a particular idea at least once. It eliminates the double counting of people who express the same idea multiple times, possibly in slightly different ways.

Norms
The average of scores taken from the database of other commercials tested in the same way, which are presumed to follow a normal or bell-shaped curve. Norms are used to provide a

benchmark for interpreting evaluative scores or diagnostic rating statements.

Offline Research

Pre-test research conducted in person, at a central location or a convenience sample of consumers intercepted at a research facility within a mall, rather than on the Internet.

Online Research

Pre-test research that is conducted over the Internet. In general, ratings collected online cannot be compared to ratings collected offline without some further adjustment factor. Experimental work to compare online with offline data collection shows that Picture Sorts are comparable for either method of data collection.

Open Ended Questions

Questions asked that are designed to collect respondent thoughts in their own words, rather than with pre-determined choices or rating statements. Communication of strategic messages is assessed by coding verbatim playback from open-ended questions. Also known as "open ends."

Panel

A group of respondents who are recruited to participate in consumer research at regular intervals over an extended time period. The two most commonly used approaches are national mail and national online panels.

PAPI

Paper and Pencil Interviewing. In this traditional approach, the respondent completes a paper questionnaire.

Peak Visuals

These are the most salient points in the visual experience of a commercial. Peak visuals are the highest recalled visuals in the local neighborhood of pictures plotted in the Flow of Attention graph. Research indicates that peak visuals are the images most likely to enter the consumer's long term memory and contribute to the long-term effects of advertising. Peak visuals can also be identified with the "beat" of the film experience, which many film editors intuitively think of as the fundamental unit of structure in film storytelling.

Persona

The human face or personality that advertising projects onto a brand. The brand persona is collected through the use of a checklist of personality traits. Some examples are Contemporary, Traditional, Friendly and Smart.

Picture Sorts®

A proprietary tool developed by Ameritest

that is used to deconstruct the audience's visual experience of a television commercial. Different Picture Sorts are used to diagnose different strengths and weaknesses of the commercial. Three types of sorts are the Flow of Attention, the Flow of Emotion and the Flow of Meaning. Special sorts are also conducted depending on potential creative issues. As a diagnostic tool, the Ameritest Picture Sorts have been validated against all the major pre-test report card measures.

Place

The emotional place where a brand lives (as distinct from semantic positioning). A brand place such as Marlboro country, or the Green Giant's valley, or the Keebler Elves' tree becomes a stage for telling a brand's stories and a mental container for storing a brand's values and memories.

Positioning

The place a brand occupies in the mind of the consumer in the context of the brand's competitive set. First popularized by Reis & Trout in their book, *Positioning*, this marketing concept deals with the semantic memory system. Because positioning is a semantic or verbal construct, a brand's positioning can easily be measured with traditional verbal rating statements in a pre-test.

Positive Transition

One of four archetypal dramatic structures identified with the Flow of Emotion. It is also known as Supporting Actor-type advertising. In this particular dramatic structure, the audience experiences a quantum leap in emotions, from a low emotion state to a high emotion state, as a function of the action of the brand.

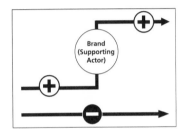

Pre-testing

Testing television commercials prior to airing them or moving them to a higher level of finish. The first goal is to qualify the ad as strong enough to meet company action standards for final production or airing. The second goal is to identify opportunities to improve the performance of the advertising through editing.

Pre-recruiting

A method of recruiting respondents by telephone and making an appointment for the respondent to be interviewed, versus recruiting respondents from the mall or street to be interviewed immediately. Pre-recruiting is often used for specific samples outside the general population that can be difficult to find, such as business professionals, physicians, etc.

Precision

Usually refers to the number of "significant digits" that are reported in decimal numbers for quantitative variables. There is a lesser need for precision in advertising research in which subjective perceptions are measured, with most practitioners sticking to one significant decimal point.

Probe

A follow-up question designed to clarify the meaning of respondent answers to a question that has just been asked.

Product Drama

The use of the power of film to promise the emotional or sensory experience a consumer might have in consuming a product. It is the role the product visuals play in creating the virtual consumption experience which is a "false memory" of a positive brand experience generated by advertising.

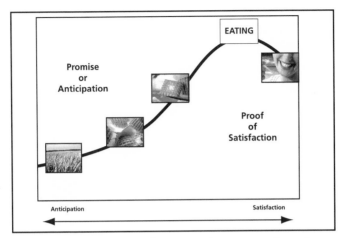

Product Drama Curve for virtual consumption of food product.

Product Narrative Integration

One of the diagnostic tests for branding is whether the respondent can play back the story of the ad in response to open-ended questions without mentioning the brand. Commercials where the product is strongly integrated into the storyline tend to be well-branded.

Product Peak

A Flow of Attention peak where the visual contains product-related content, such as a package shot, product in use, product demo, etc. Ads that test well in Day-After Recall testing systems tend to have a high proportion of product peaks compared to executional peaks, which indicates a focus on rational rather than emotional communication.

Purchase Intent

A standard five-point purchase intent scale, ranging from "definitely will buy", "probably will buy" to "definitely will not buy," which is usually weighted to count the "definitely will buy" rating most heavily toward measuring the persuasiveness of advertising.

Reach

A media measure reporting the proportion of the target audience that is exposed *at least once* to your advertising message during a given time period. This is the companion concept to media "frequency." The concepts of reach and frequency take account of the breadth and the depth of the advertising media buy.

Reliability

Relates to consistency of measurement. For example, all other things being equal, a commercial that is retested in a given system should receive similar scores on the second test as on the first. Most major pre-testing systems have test-retest reliability scores of over 90%.

Rotation

The practice of varying the order of stimuli so that there is no systematic preference based on what was shown first or last. Ideally, each respondent is shown stimuli in a different random order.

Sample

Those members of a population you survey in order to draw conclusions about the larger population of which those respondents are members.

Scatterplot

This is a visual representation of quantitative data shown as points on a plane.

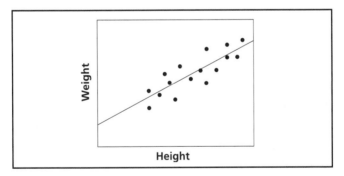

Example of a Scatterplot.

Screening Questions

These are questions asked before the main questionnaire to determine eligibility of the consumer to participate in the research study as a respondent. At the very least, consumers are screened out for "security purposes"—if they work in advertising/marketing or, alternatively, in an industry that relates to the brands, products, consumer research, or services being focused upon in a given study.

Selling-Edge Analysis

A quantitative technique that uses brand ratings from a copytest to identify the degree to which different product attributes or benefits are driving purchase motivation after removing any halo effects. Also used to validate the underlying strategy of the advertising.

Semantic Information

The rational informational content of an ad, such as selling propositions, product facts, or other functional product information. Semantic information is translatable from one channel of communication to another. It is, for example, the part of a picture a respondent can talk about. Consequently, the communication of semantic information can be tested with traditional verbal methods. This is the part of the commercial message that plugs into the semantic memory system.

Semantic Memory

One of several memory systems in the mind. This is the system where logical, structured concepts related to the outside world are stored (in contrast to the Episodic memory system). It is the part of the brain where a brand's place in the world, or positioning, is established. This system is easily accessed via verbal research techniques and is the basis for traditional pre-testing methods.

Semantic Network

A quantitative technique that analyzes the data in a control and test cell to determine how an ad strengthens the linkages between related ideas in a product category. This technique can also be used as a tool for strategy development for identifying different "selling pathways" for motivating the consumer.

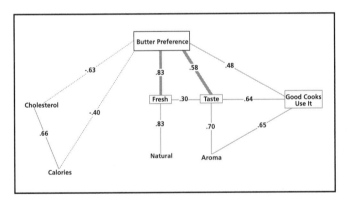

Example of a Semantic Network for butter.

Simulated Test Market

This is a type of concept research study used to predict year one sales or market share for a new product or service based on consumer response to an ad, either in rough or final form, in combination with other marketing and media plan assumptions. The most widely used simulated test market system is BASES.

Single-Minded Branding Moment

A Flow of Attention peak that contains a single focus of attention on the identity of the brand being advertised. It is distinguished from branding peaks where audience attention may be divided between the brand name and other distracting executional elements competing for attention within the frame.

Skin Conductance

Another physiological measure of emotional arousal that is sometimes used to measure the emotional response to advertising. Changes in skin conductivity to electrical currents is also the basis for polygraphs or "lie detectors."

Spontaneous Playback

Respondent mentions of an idea contained in the commercial without prompting or probing by the interview. Spontaneous playback suggests that an idea is "top-of-mind." It is a better indicator of commercial effectiveness than ideas extracted from the consumer through probing.

Statistical Test of Significance

This is an analytical method used to determine if the difference you observe between two pre-tests, for example, is a chance difference or a real difference. When the difference is very slight, this method will tell you that it is over-whelmingly due to chance factors. Alternative-ly, when the difference is very large, this method will tell you that it's not likely due to chance factors. Therefore, it's a real difference. It is customary to conduct two types of statisti-cal tests of significance: (1) between pre-test results of different ads on key performance measures and (2) between a pre-test result for an ad and its corresponding norm.

Stealomatic/Ripomatic

A "rough" television commercial created by joining together "borrowed" pieces of pre-existing film (e.g., from director's reels) for the purpose of testing an advertising concept. This type of commercial may be indistinguishable from a finished film commercial from the viewer's standpoint, but it is far less expensive to produce than film created from scratch.

Stickiness

A diagnostic measure that captures the extent to which viewers wish to spend more time looking at or reading a print ad. This measure is used to help understand a print ad's performance on the key evaluative measures of Stopping Power and Brand Linkage. However, there are no absolute levels of stickiness required for advertising effectiveness. For example, a visually simple ad with little copy could be a "quick read", but nevertheless be quite effective.

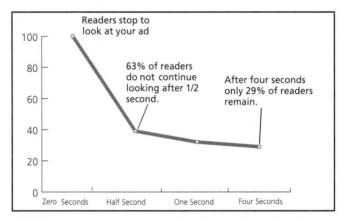

Stickiness is a measure of the decay of readership over time.

Stopping Power

Another name for an Attention Score for print ads. Conceptually, this is the ability of a print ad to break through a cluttered media environment and grab the attention of the reader—i.e. to stop the reader from flipping past the page the ad is on.

Storyboard

A "comic strip" style page consisting of the key frames in a television commercial along with frame-by-frame notations for copy and sound effects.

Stubs

All of the rows that run vertically down the side of a page in a cross-tabulation. The stubs are usually the dependent variables in a study.

Subjective Time

In contrast to mechanical clock time, subjective time is the idea that the perception of time (time flying by us, time dragging slowly) is tied to experience. Subjective time is tied to the rate of information flow in an ad, e.g., cutting speed. Picture sorts, with a variable number of pictures used to describe the visual information content in different ads, use subjective time as the frame of reference for measuring the ad experience, as opposed to dial-a-meter approaches which use clock time, e.g., every 0.2 seconds, for measurement. This is one

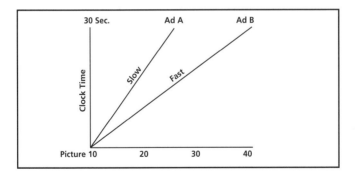

Ad B produces a more energetic, perceived subjective time than ad A because of the higher rate of information flow.

reason the two approaches produce fundamentally different insights.

Sustained Emotion

One of four archetypal dramatic structures identified with the Flow of Emotion. It is also known as Producer-type advertising. This dramatic structure is characterized by a high level of continuous positive emotions with no negatives. The brand is usually introduced early in the commercial as the presenter or source of these emotions. Montage commercials with strong music soundtracks are an example of this type of advertising. When the content of the ad is rational product information, rather than emotional content, this type of execution turns into a lecture type of ad.

Tab Plan

A detailed specification of the various banner points and stubs to be used in processing cross-tabulations from a research study.

Target Rating Points (TRPs)

Same as GRPs, but the base is the *target audience* you are trying to reach rather than all the households in the market. It's a measure of the total media weight spent to reach this target, measured as the product of both Reach and Frequency.

Thinking

The use of cognitive processes (e.g., encoding, storing and retrieving) that are put into service in reacting to stimuli in the outside world, or as a result of other related thoughts that come into consciousness (e.g., beliefs, attitudes, and evaluations).

Top Box

The percentage of a sample choosing the highest rating on a scale. Top box ratings are an indicator of the intensity of consumer feelings or perceptions, and generally are more discriminating measures than mean scores. For example, validation research by concept-testing companies has shown repeatedly that top box purchase intent carries the most weight in actually predicting consumer purchase behavior.

Topline

This is also referred to as a topline report. In general, this is a summary of the key performance scores or evaluative measures, without the diagnostics or analysis.

Trace

Millward Brown's moment-by-moment technique using a one dimensional, dial-a-meter response to TV commercials. A number of experiments have shown that Trace and Picture Sorts produce results that are uncorrelated, so the two approaches seem to be measuring very different things.

Validity

This concept deals with the question of whether or not you are actually measuring what you say it is you are measuring. For example, is day-after recall in advertising research really a measure of breakthrough? These days, all the major copytesting systems claim substantial evidence supporting the relationship between in-market sales effects and their key measures, so validity is a "cost of entry" criterion for using any pre-testing system.

Example of a Validation graph from Ameritest.

Values

The axiomatic set of ideas which determine a person's life. Frequently the values people claim to hold are different from their true or underlying values. According to screenwriter Robert McKee, people reveal their true values by the choices they make under pressure. Brands can usually own only one or a few values in the mind of the consumer, usually through the brand-building process of advertising. For example, Coca-Cola tries to own the value of authenticity, the "real thing." Marlboro cigarettes tries to own the values of freedom and independence through its long lasting "Marlboro Country" campaign.

Verbatims

The respondent's answers, recorded word for word, to open-end questions in the interview. Selective use of verbatims in the research report can sometimes illuminate insights into how the advertising concept is perceived by the audience.

Video Rhythm

The natural wave-like curve one expects to see in the Flow of Attention that reflects the interaction between audience and film. This curve occurs because the human mind can only process visual information at a certain speed and so consumes information in meaningful chunks. These chunks are equivalent to peak moments, the fundamental units of structure in film storytelling.

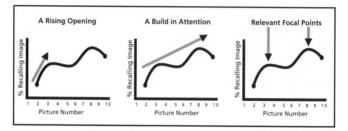

Characteristics of a Flow of Attention curve related to Attention and Recall.

Viral Marketing

Viral Marketing describes any strategy that encourages individuals to pass on a marketing message to others, creating potential for exponential growth in the message's exposure and influence.

Virtual Consumption

A theory about how advertising works that explains the important role that experiential product drama plays. Because memories stored in the episodic memory system are easily rewritten or revised, it is hypothesized that the artificial or "false" memories created by advertising are mixed together with the real memories of product experience to create brand loyalty. For example, a consumer who has four real brand experiences in a year and sees advertising for that brand six more times will have memories of ten brand experiences a year. In analyzing advertising, therefore, it is important to understand how the film dramatizes the virtual consumption experience of the brand.

Visual Connectedness

The extent to which the Flow of Attention pattern is smooth and continuous as opposed to scattered, turbulent or disjointed. This is a measure of how well the images in the commercial are glued together in the mind of the viewer. Smooth flows, which indicate stronger connections being made between the images in a commercial, are characteristic of more persuasive commercials.

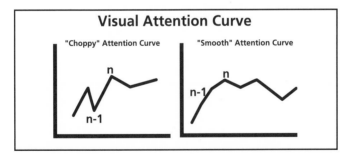

Persuasive ads tend to exhibit smoother flows, or be better connected.

Warm-Up Questions

These are interesting, simple, and non-threatening questions (e.g., "What are your favorite television shows?") posed at the beginning of the interview (after the screening questions) and are designed to get the consumer into the "mind-set" of being a respondent. The responses to these types of questions are usually not analyzed.

Wear-In
This is the notion that up to a point the selling power of advertising *builds* over time and with repeated exposures.

Wear-Out
This is the notion that up to a point the selling power of advertising *declines* over time and with repeated exposures.

Working Emotion
This is also known as "aesthetic emotion"—the reactions Aristotle says are produced by works of art. An analogy to working energy in physics, this concept divides the emotional content of advertising into two categories: the emotion created by a commercial that is put to work for the brand in persuading or selling the product versus borrowed interest, or the entertainment values that only work to attract attention to the advertising execution. The strong correlation between the Flow of Emotion and Motivation suggests that the Flow of Emotion is a good measure of Working Emotion.

XI
Resources

XI

Resources

WEBSITES

AAAA American Association of Advertising Agencies, www.aaaa.org

AAPOR American Association for Public Opinion Research www.aapor.org

ACR Association for Consumer Research www.acrweb.org

ADM American Demographics Magazine www.demographics.com

AMA American Marketing Association www.marketingpower.com

Ameritest advertising research firm www.ameritest.net

ARF Advertising Research Foundation www.thearf.org

ASA American Statistical Association www.amstat.org

CASRO Council of American Survey Research Organizations www.casro.org

CMOR Council for Marketing and Opinion Research www.cmor.org

ESOMAR European Society of Opinion and Marketing Research www.esomar.org

McKee, Robert World-renowned expert on story-telling and creator of the Story seminar www.mckeestory.com

MRA Marketing Research Association www.mra-net.org

Quirk's Marketing Research Review Magazine www.quirks.com

QRCA Qualitative Research Consultants Association www.qrca.org

The Santa Fe Institute A multidisciplinary research and education center, pursuing emerging science www.santafe.edu

Tufte, Edward R. Data artist www.edwardtufte.com/tufte

US Census Bureau www.census.gov

WARC World Advertising Research Center, Ltd. Home of **Admap** magazine. www.warc.com

NOTES

[1]Brown, G. *Insights into Campaign Wear-in and Wear-out from Continuous Tracking*. Paper presented at the ARF Advertising Tracking Studies Workshop, New York, 1984.

[2]Brown, G. *Campaign Tracking: New Learning on Copy Evaluation and Wearout*. Paper presented at the Fourth Annual ARF Copy Research Workshop, New York, 1987.

[3]Ostlund, L. E., Clancy, K. J., and Sapra, R. Inertia in Copy Research. *Journal of Advertising Research*, 1980, 20(1), 17–23.

[4]Honomichl, J. J. *Honomichl on Marketing Research*. Lincolnwood, IL: NTC Business Books, 1986.

[5]Ross, H. Recall vs. Persuasion: An Answer. *Journal of Advertising Research*, 1982, 22(1), 13–16.

[6]Lodish, L. M., Abraham, M., Kalmenson, S., Livelsberger, J., Lubetkin, B., Richardson, B., & Stevens, M. E. How TV Advertising Works: A Meta-Analysis of 389 Real World Split Cable TV Advertising Experiments. *Journal of Marketing Research*, May 1995, 125–139.

[7]Schwerin, Horace S., and Henry H. Newel,

Persuasion in Marketing, John Wiley and Sons, Inc., April, 1981.

[8]Blair, M. H. An Empirical Investigation of Advertising Wearin and Wearout. *Journal of Advertising Research*, 40 (November/December 2000).

[9]Arnold, S. J., & Bird, J. R. The Day After Recall Test of Advertising Effectiveness: A Discussion of the Issues. In *Current Issues and Research in Advertising*, 1982, 59–68.

[10]Young, C. E. The Eye Is Not A Camera. *Quirk's Marketing Research Review*, 2003, 58–63.

[11]Young, C. E. Researcher as Teacher: A Heuristic Model for Pre-Testing TV Commercials. *Quirk's Marketing Research Review*, 2001, 23–27.

[12]Kastenholz, J., Young, C., & Kerr, G. Does Day-After Recall Testing Produce Vanilla Advertising? *Admap*, June 2004, 34–36.

[13]Kastenholz, J., Kerr, G., & Young, C. Focus and Fit: Advertising and Branding Join Forces to Create a Star. *Marketing Research*, Spring 2004, 16–21.

[14]Moult, W. H. *Selective Success Amid Chaos: Advertising in the 1990s.* Paper presented at Esomar, 1995. In *Selected Papers and Presentations: 1990-1996*, Stamford, CT.: ASI Market Research, Inc., 1996.

[15]Wells, W. D., Leavitt, C., and McConville, M. A Reaction Profile for TV Commercials. *Journal of Advertising Research*, 11(6), December 1971, 11–17.

[16]Schlinger, M. J. A Profile of Responses to Commercials. *Journal of Advertising Research*, 1979, 19(2), 37–46.

[17]Krugman, H. Memory Without Recall, Exposure Without Perception. *Journal of Advertising Research*, July/August, 1977.

[18]Hall, B. F. A New Model for Measuring Advertising Effectiveness. *Journal of Advertising Research*, March/April 2002, 23–31.

[19]Young, C. E., & Robinson, M. Video Rhythms and Recall. *Journal of Advertising Research*, June/July 1989, 22–25.

[20]Young, C. E., & Robinson, M. Visual Connectedness and Persuasion. *Journal of Advertising Research*, March/April 1992, 51–59.

[21]Young, C. E., & Kastenholz, J. Emotion in TV Ads. *Admap*, 2004, 40–42.

[21]Young, C. E. Brain Waves, Picture Sorts, and Branding Moments. *Journal of Advertising Research*, 42(4), 2002, 42–53.

[23]Young, C. E. Capturing the Flow of Emotion in Television Commercials: A New Approach. *Journal of Advertising Research*, June 2004, 202–209.

[24]Zaltman, G. (2003), *How Customers Think: Essential Insights Into the Mind of the Market*, Boston, MA: Harvard Business School Press.

PUBLICATIONS

Aaker, D. A., *Building Strong Brands*. New York, NY: The Free Press, 1996.

Agres, S. J., Edell, J. A., & Dubitsky, T. M. *Emotion in Advertising: Theoretical and Practical Explorations*. Westport, CT: Quorum Books, 1990.

American Association of Advertising Agencies. Positioning Advertising Copy Testing (PACT): A Consensus Credo Representing the Views of Leading American Advertising Agencies. NY: AAAA, 1982.

Arnheim, R., *Visual Thinking*, Berkeley: University of California Press, 1974.

Arnold, S. J., & Bird, J. R. The Day-After Recall Test of Advertising Effectiveness: A Discussion of the Issues. In *Current Issues and Research in Advertising*, 1982, 59–68.

Blair, M. H., An empirical investigation of advertising wearin and wearout. *Journal of Advertising Research*, 2000, 40(6), 95–104.

Bohm, D., *On Dialogue*, London: Routeledge, 1996.

Booth, W., *A Rhetoric of Irony*, Chicago: University of Chicago Press, 1974.

Brown, G., Campaign Tracking: New Learning on Copy Evaluation and Wearout. Paper presented at the Fourth Annual ARF Copy Research Workshop, New York, 1987.

Brown, G., Insights into Campaign Wear-in and Wear-out from Continuous Tracking. Paper presented at the ARF Advertising Tracking Studies Workshop, New York, 1984.

Campbell, D. T., & Stanley, J. C., *Experimental and Quasi-Experimental Designs for Research*. Chicago, IL: Rand McNally, 1963.

Campbell, J., *Grammatical Man*, New York: Simon and Schuster, 1982.

Csikszentmihalyl, M., *Flow: The Psychology of Optimal Experience*, New York: Harper Collins, 1990.

Ehrenberg, A. S. C., Repetitive advertising and the consumer. *Journal of Avertising Research*, 2000, 40(6), 39–49.

Einstein, S., *Film Form*, New York: Harcourt Brace, 1977.

Eisner, W., *Graphic Storytelling*, Tamarac, Florida: Poorhouse Press, 1996.

Fryer, B., Storytelling that Moves People: A Conversation with Screenwriting Coach Robert Mckee. *Harvard Business Review*, June 2003.

Gigerenzer, G., and Todd, P., *Simple*

Heuristics That Make Us Smart, Oxford University Press, 1999.

Gladwell, M., *Blink.*, New York: Little, Brown, 2005.

Gladwell, M., *The Tipping Point.* New York: Back Bay Books, 2002.

Goffman, E., *The Presentation of Self in Everyday Life*, Garden City, NY: Doubleday, 1959.

Greenspan, S. I., & Shanker, S. G. *The First Idea: How Symbols, Language, and Intelligence Evolved from our Primate Ancestors to Modern Humans*. Cambridge, MA: DaCapo Press, 2004.

Grobe, M., *Emotional Branding: The New Paradigm for Connecting Brands to People*. New York, NY: Allworth Press, 2001.

Haley, R. I., & Baldinger, A. L. The ARF Copy Research Validity Project. *Journal of Advertising Research*, 2000, 40(6), 114–136.

Hall, B. F., A New Model for Measuring Advertising Effectiveness. *Journal of Advertising Research*, March/April 2002, 23–31.

Hall, B. F, On measuring the power of communications. *Journal of Advertising Research*, 2004, 44(2), June, 181–188.

Hoffman, D., *Visual Intelligence*, New York: Norton, 1998.

Holland, J., *Hidden Order*, Cambridge, MA: Helix, 1995.

Honomichl, J. J., *Honomichl on Marketing Research.* Lincolnwood, IL: NTC Business Books, 1986.

Jones, J. P., *What's in a Name: Advertising and the Concept of Brands.* Lexington, MA: D. C. Heath Books, 1986.

Jones, J. P., (Editor), *How Advertising Works: The Role of Research.* Thousand Oaks, CA: Sage Publications, 1998.

Kastenholz, J., Kerr, G., & Young, C., Focus and Fit: Advertising and Branding Join Forces to Create a Star. *Marketing Research*, Spring 2004, 16–21.

Kastenholz, J., Young, C., & Dubitsky, T., Roughing It: Rehearse Your Creative Ideas in Rough Production to Optimize Ad Effectiveness. *Marketing Research*, 2004 (Winter), 16(4), 22–27.

Kastenholz, J., Young, C., A Film Director's Guide to Ad Effectiveness. *Admap*, September 2003.

Kastenholz, J., Young, C., & Kerr, G., Does Day-After Recall Testing Produce Vanilla

Advertising? *Admap*, June 2004, 34–36.

Klapp, O., *Heroes, Villains and Fools*, Englewood Cliffs, NJ: Prentice-Hall, 1962.

Krugman, H., Memory Without Recall, Exposure Without Perception. *Journal of Advertising Research*, July/August, 1977.

Krugman, H. E., Memory without recall, exposure without perception. *Journal of Advertising Research*, 2000, 40(6), 49–54.

Kuhns, W., *The Moving Picture Book*. Dayton, OH: Pflaum, 1975.

Leahey, T. J., & Harris, R. J. *Human Learning*. Englewood Cliffs, NJ: Prentice-Hall, 1985.

Lodish, L. M., Abraham, M., Kalmenson, S., Livelsberger, J., Lubetkin, B., Richardson, B., & Stevens, M. E., How TV Advertising Works: A Meta-Analysis of 389 Real World Split Cable TV Advertising Experiments. *Journal of Marketing Research*, May 1995, 125–139.

Malhotra, N. K., *Marketing Research: An Applied Orientation*. (3rd Edition.) Upper Saddle River, NJ: Prentice-Hall, 1999.

Maloney, J. C., Curiosity versus disbelief in advertising. *Journal of Advertising Research*, 2000, 40(6), 7–14.

McCloud, Scott, *Understanding Comics: The invisible art*. New York, NY: Harper Collins, 1993.

McKee, Robert, *Story: Substance, Structure, Style and the Principles of Screenwriting*. NY, NY: HarperCollins Books, 1997.

Meyrowitz, J., *No Sense of Place*, Oxford: Oxford University Press, 1985.

Moles, A., *Information Theory and Esthetic Perception*, Urbana: University of Illinois Press, 1967.

Moult, W. H., Selective Success Amid Chaos: Advertising in the 1990s. Paper presented at Esomar, 1995. In *Selected Papers and Presentations*: 1990–1996, Stamford, CT.: ASI Market Research, Inc., 1996.

Murch, Walter, *In the blink of an eye*, Beaverly Hills, CA, Silman-James press, 2001.

Ondaatje, Michael, *The Conversations: Walter Murch and the Art of Editing Film*, New York, NY: Alfred Al. Knopf, 2002.

Ostlund, L. E., Clancy, K. J., and Sapra, R. Inertia in Copy Research. *Journal of Advertising Research*, 1980, 20(1), 17–23.

Plummer, J. T., How personality makes a difference. *Journal of Advertising Research*, 2000, 40(6), 79–84.

Ries, A., & Trout, J., *Positioning: The Battle For Your Mind*, New York, NY: McGraw-Hill, 2000.

Ries, A., & Trout, J., *The 22 Immutable Laws*

of Marketing. New York, NY: Harper Collins, 1994.

Ross, H., Recall vs. Persuasion: An Answer. *Journal of Advertising Research*, 1982, 22(1), 13–16.

Schlinger, M. J., A Profile of Responses to Commercials. *Journal of Advertising Research*, 1979, 19(2), 37–46.

Schlinger, M. J., Olson, D., and Young, C., How Consumers React to New-Product Ads, *Journal of Advertising Research,* June/July, 1982, Vol 2, No 3.

Scott, D. R., & Solomon, D., What is wearout anyway? *Journal of Advertising Research*, 1998, 38(5), 19–28.

Senge, P., *The Fifth Discipline*, new York: Doubleday, 1990.

Shannon, C., and Weaver, W., *The Mathematical Theory of Communication*, Urbana: University of Illinois Press, 1975.

Stewart, D. W., & Furse, D. H., Analysis of the impact of executional factors on advertising performance. *Journal of Advertising Research*, 1984, 24 (December), 23–26.

Stewart, D. W., & Furse, D. H., *Effective Television Advertising: A Study of 1,000 Commercials*. Lexington, MA: D. C. Heath Books, 1986.

Surmanek, J., *Media Planning: A Practical Guide*. (3rd Edition.) Chicago, IL: NTC Business Books, 1996.

Sutherland, M., & Sylvester, A., *Advertising and the Mind of the Consumer: What Works, What Doesn't and Why*. St. Leonards, Australia: Allen & Unwin Press, 2000.

Tabachnick, B. G., & Fidell, L. S., *Using Multivariate Statistics*. New York, NY: Harper & Row, 1983.

Tufte, Edward R., *Envisioning Information*. Cheshire, CT: Graphics Press, 1990.

Tufte, Edward R., *The Visual Display of Quantitative Information*. (2nd Edition.) Cheshire, CT: Graphics Press, 2001.

Tufte, Edward R., *Visual Explanations*. Cheshire, CT: Graphics Press, 1997.

Tulving, E., *The Elements of Episodic Memory*, Oxford: Oxford University Press, 1983.

Wells, W. D., Lectures and Dramas, *Cognitive and Affective Responses to Advertising*. Lexington Books: Mass./Toronto, 1988.

Wells, W. D., Leavitt, C., and McConville, M. A, Reaction Profile for TV Commercials. *Journal of Advertising Research*, 11(6), December 1971, 11–17.

Young, C., Brain Waves, Picture Sorts, and Branding Moments. *Journal of Advertising Research*, 42(4), 2002, 42–53.

Young, C., The Eye Is Not A Camera. *Quirk's Marketing Research Review*, 2003, 58–63.

Young, C., Capturing the Flow of Emotion in Television Commercials: A New Approach. *Journal of Advertising Research*, June 2004, 202–209.

Young, C. E., Researcher as Teacher: A Heuristic Model for Pre-Testing TV Commercials. *Quirks Marketing Research Review*, 2001, 23–27.

Young, C. E., & Robinson, M., Video Rhythms and Recall. *Journal of Advertising Research*, June/July 1989, 22–25.

Young, C. E., & Robinson, M. Visual Connectedness and Persuasion. *Journal of Advertising Research*, March/April 1992, 51–59.

Young, C., & Kastenholz, J. Emotion in TV Ads. *Admap*, 2004, 40–42.

Zaltman, G., *How Customers Think: Essential Insights into the Mind of the Market.* Boston, MA: Harvard Business School Press, 2003.

Rough Guide to Statistical Testing

One of the questions frequently asked in any research meeting with numbers is, "Is that difference significant?" For example, if your ad generates a 52 Attention score and another ad generates a 40, how do you determine if your ads Attention score is *significantly* different from the other ad?

What follows is a convenient method to determine very quickly (*without* using any statistical formulas) whether certain differences in a pre-testing report are statistically significant.

Perhaps the most useful comparison will be between a test cell and a norm. You'll want to know whether your ad scored significantly above or below a given norm for a key evaluative measure. Another useful comparison will be between two ads that have been pre-tested (i.e., between two test cells). For instance, you'll want to know whether one ad is outperforming the other on a key evaluative measure. The chart shown below assumes that the sample sizes for your test cells are equal to 125.

You may also want to determine whether

	Sample Size 1st Ad 125	Norm	Sample Size 1st Ad 125	Sample Size 2nd Ad 125
Approximate minimum percent difference needed for statistical significance at 90% confidence level.	8%		10%	

your ad performs differently for one specific
target group segment compared to another
target group segment. Listed below are approx-
imate minimum percent differences that would
correspond to analysis of subsets of your total
dataset.

	Sample Size 1st Ad 60	Sample Size 2nd Ad 60	Sample Size 1st Ad 50	Sample Size 2nd Ad 75
Approximate minimum percent difference needed for statistical significance at 90% confidence level.	14%		13%	

	Sample Size 1st Ad 25	Sample Size 2nd Ad 100	Sample Size 1st Ad 30	Sample Size 2nd Ad 90
Approximate minimum percent difference needed for statistical significance at 90% confidence level.	20%		16%	